CULTURE SMART!

ICELAND

THE ESSENTIAL GUIDE TO CUSTOMS & CULTURE

THORGEIR FREYR SVEINSSON

KUPERARD

"The real voyage of discovery consists not in seeking new landscapes, but in having new eyes."

Adapted from Marcel Proust, *Remembrance of Things Past*.

ISBN 978 1 78702 904 0
British Library Cataloguing in Publication Data
A CIP catalogue entry for this book is available
from the British Library

First published in Great Britain
by Kuperard, an imprint of Bravo Ltd
59 Hutton Grove, London N12 8DS
Tel: +44 (0) 20 8446 2440
www.culturesmart.co.uk
Inquiries: publicity@kuperard.co.uk

Design Bobby Birchall
Printed in Turkey by Elma Basim

The Culture Smart! series is continuing to expand.
All Culture Smart! guides are available as e-books, and many
as audio books. For further information and latest titles visit
www.culturesmart.co.uk

THORGEIR FREYR SVEINSSON is a native Icelander hailing from the northwestern settlement of Skagafjörður. He holds a Cand.theol. in Theology from the University of Iceland, and a Master's in Management from Birkbeck College, University of London. Like a true Norseman, Thorgeir has laid anchor in Norway, Finland, and the United Kingdom and is well practiced in the art of navigating new cultures. A keen angler and soccer fan, for a time he ran a guesthouse with his wife in Selfoss, southern Iceland. Today he and his wife live in Reykjavik, where he works as a project manager at the University of Iceland.

CONTENTS

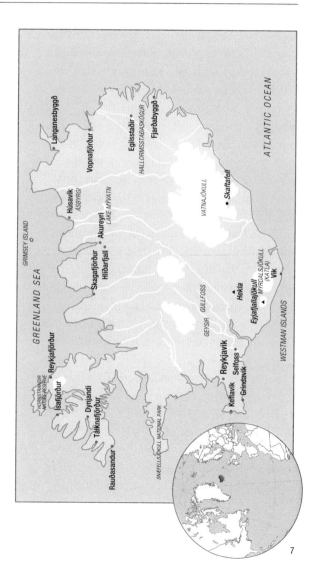

INTRODUCTION

Iceland has erupted onto the travel scene in recent years. With striking views of bubbling turquoise geysers set among rugged snowy peaks, black sand beaches, crashing glacial waterfalls, and the ethereal majesty of the northern lights, one can only wonder what took it so long. But what of the people who call this remote North Atlantic island home? Behind a stoic veneer lies a proud, industrious, and egalitarian people, whose straightforwardness and ability to wing it have seen them thrive in this beautiful but unforgiving environment.

The first settlers to arrive in the ninth century were Vikings fleeing the King of Norway who sought to bring them under his rule. Despite the harsh terrain and extreme isolation of their refuge, these anti-authoritarian Norsemen succeeded in settling the island. The society that developed there counts itself today among the most affluent and progressive in the world. Fresh spring water flows from the faucets of every home, while the country's abundant geothermal stores provide heating and hot water for all.

Icelanders are highly educated, most own their own homes, crime rates are close to nonexistent, and a comprehensive welfare system stands ready to support those who may fall on hard times. How was this achieved, and what kind of philosophical armory was forged in the long winters that have enabled them not just to survive, but to thrive?

Central to the Icelandic way of life is the concept of *thetta reddast*. Translated roughly, it means "everything will work out fine," and reflects the basic optimism that pervades everything an Icelander does, even if this isn't necessarily accompanied by a smile. *Thetta reddast* promotes a readiness and flexibility of response in the face of life's challenges, and it has proved its worth in countless situations, from volcanic eruptions to economic crashes. This attitude has its downsides too, though; an aversion to forward planning can mean having to deal with problems that could otherwise have been foreseen and avoided.

The stubborn self-reliance of their forebears, too, has served them well, as has the supreme value given to independence, kept alive despite centuries of foreign rule. It explains why children are given responsibilities from an early age, why workplace seniority buys little in the way of deference, and why the country has repeatedly refused to join the European Union. Instead, authority is treated with a mixture of suspicion and derision.

Culture Smart! Iceland will equip you with a deeper understanding of your hosts and their complexities, as well as with vital insights to turn your visit into a more enriching experience. Throughout the book place names have been written in Icelandic so that they can be more easily identified on local roadsigns and maps. A guide to the pronunciation of Icelandic's Old Norse letters is given on page 178.

Official Name	Iceland	*Ísland*
Population	Iceland 360,000.	Most sparsely populated country in Europe. Around 80% of the country remains uninhabited
Area	40,000 square miles (103,000 square kilometers).	Comparable in size to the state of Tennessee.
Capital City	Reykjavik (Reykjavík). Population 131,000	Translates as "Bay of Smokes" in Old Norse.
Other Main Towns	Akureyri in the northeast, Arborg in the south, Fjardabyggd in the east.	Reykjavik capital region includes towns of Kopavogur, Hafnarfjordur, and Gardabaer.
Terrain	Mountain peaks and fertile lowlands. 11% of Iceland is covered by glaciers. Approximately 130 volcanoes, many buried deep below glacial ice.	Located atop the Mid-Atlantic Ridge, Iceland is growing at the rate of 5 cm per year as the Eurasian and North American tectonic plates shift apart.
Climate	Temperate. Long winters and short summers. Snow fall can be expected from October to April.	Gulf Stream maintains mild temperatures year round. Weather is extremely changeable.
Currency	Icelandic krona (crown)	ISK
Language	Icelandic. Most are also fluent in English and one or more of the other Nordic languages.	
Ethnic Makeup	North Germanic. Most Icelanders descend from early Norwegian settlers as well as slaves taken from Scotland and Ireland.	

Life Expectancy	Total population: 83; Male: 81; Female: 85	
Age Structure	0-14 years: 20.31%; 15-24 years: 12.85%; 25-54 years: 39.44%; 55-64 years: 11.94%; 65 years and over: 15.47%	
Religion	Lutheran Church of Iceland 63.4%, Other non-Catholic Churches 7.4%, Roman Catholic 4.2%	Asatru 1.31%, other and unspecified 14.3%, unaffiliated 7.17%
Government	Parliament is called The Althing; a unicameral legislature. Multi-party majority rule system with elections held every 4 years.	Elections have been more frequent In recent years, due to political unrest following the economic crash of 2008.
Economy	Combination of capitalist and free-market economy with comprehensive welfare system.	Main exports include fish products, tourism, aluminum, as well as software, silicone, and woolen goods.
Resources	Natural resources supply 85% of domestic energy needs.	100% of electricity and heat from renewable sources, including geothermal heat and hydropower.
Telephone	+354	Emergency services 112
Time	GMT (UTC)	
Electricity	230V (50Hz)	Two-pronged plugs
Media	Main TV channel is RÚV (state-owned and tax funded).	*Fréttablaðið* and *Morgunblaðið* are the two most widely circulated newspapers.
Internet	.is	

CHAPTER ONE

LAND *&* PEOPLE

Iceland is situated in the northern reaches of the Atlantic Ocean, halfway between the continents of Europe and North America. It is a comparatively young island, formed by the collision of the Eurasian and North American tectonic plates some eighteen million years ago. Today those tectonic plates are shifting apart. The magma that rises from deep below the Earth's crust as a result means that Iceland's landmass is growing by roughly two inches (5 cm) every year.

Iceland is extremely isolated. Its nearest neighbor to the east is Norway, some 560 miles (900 km) away, while Greenland lies 115 miles (185 km) westward. Comparable in size to Portugal, or the state of Virginia, Iceland is home to more than 130 volcanoes, and a further 10 percent of its landmass is covered by glaciers so enormous that they are visible from space. Nearly 80 percent of the country remains uninhabited, with over two-thirds of the population concentrated in and

The steaming geothermal landscape of the Kerlingarfjöll mountain range.

around the capital, Reykjavik, in the south. Aside
from glaciers and volcanoes, Iceland is home to an
abundance of natural wonders, including bubbling
geothermal springs, icy waterfalls, glacial lagoons,
and dark, towering mountains.

CLIMATE

Iceland's climate is rather more temperate than its
name suggests. Protected by the warming currents
of the Gulf Stream, the country is spared the harsher
winter conditions that its latitude would otherwise

Goðafoss waterfall in northern Iceland.

dictate. The climate is subarctic, as opposed to arctic, with long, comparatively mild winters from September to March. At this time of year the days are short, with only three to four hours of sunlight, and average temperatures of 28° to 32°F (-2° to 0°C), depending on how far north you are, or how high. The spring and summer months, approximately April to August, are damp and cool, with an average temperature of around 55°F (13°C) and highs of 68° to 77°F (20° to 25°C). Don't let the averages fool you, though—if you are in Iceland in the winter you should expect far lower temperatures at times, so be prepared. Weather conditions in Iceland are also notoriously changeable, so whatever time of year you visit, make sure you pack a coat and layers for warmth.

DEMOGRAPHY

Iceland has a population of approximately 350,000 people, the majority of whom are the descendants of Norse settlers who arrived in the country from Norway from the ninth century onward. The seafaring Vikings brought with them slaves and servants captured on raids on the northern British Isles, and so ancestry from Ireland and Scotland is also common; it is estimated that up to 60 percent of the female settler-era population were of Celtic origin. The nation remained largely homogeneous until the twentieth century, when the economic need for manpower saw a considerable increase in foreign migrants. Today, approximately 15 percent of Iceland's population is made up of migrants, the largest communities of which include Poles, Lithuanians, and migrants from the Iberian Peninsula.

A BRIEF HISTORY

The age of settlement in Iceland began in the second half of the ninth century, when Norse settlers migrated west across the Atlantic from Norway. Although their principal reason for doing so remains the subject of debate, most scholars agree that domestic political factors in Norway played an integral role. Attempts by the Norwegian monarch, King Harald I, to unite the country under his rule were only partially successful and, as a result, the chieftains and tribal leaders who were not willing to accept subjugation set sail for new pastures. Some arrived in Iceland, though the earliest attempts at inhabiting the island by Viking explorers were ultimately unsuccessful—the extreme natural environment rendered survival a challenge beyond their means.

The arrival of the first Viking settlers in Iceland, as depicted by Norweigan painter Oscar Wergeland.

> ### *BOOK OF THE ICELANDERS*
>
> The oldest written account of Iceland's
> settlement and early national history is the
> *Íslendingabók*, ("Book of the Icelanders"),
> authored by the chronicler and priest Ari Frodi
> Thorgillson in the eleventh century. The book
> gives an account of the key settlers who arrived
> on the island and where they settled. It details
> the first lawgiving, the establishment of the
> Althing (the Icelandic parliament), the division
> of the country into quarters, and the discovery
> of Greenland. It also describes the inception
> and growth of the Icelandic Church and its
> influence.

Among the first explorers to arrive was Floki
Vilgerdarson, who is credited with giving Iceland its
name. After having arrived during the summer time,
he was unprepared when winter struck. He too found
the challenge insurmountable and returned to Norway
later the same year. To Floki's credit, he didn't give up
so easily and, though once having declared the island
worthless, he later returned and remained there until
his death.

The Sagas

The Icelandic Sagas are a unique contribution to Western literature. Remarkable for their realism, objective style, and tragic dignity, they recount the lives of the island's early settlers: farmers and fighters, poets and lovers, warriors, chieftains, and explorers.

The stand-alone stories portray historical events that are thought to have taken place at the turn of the first millennium. The authors of the Sagas are not known; many today believe that the stories formed part of a pre-existing oral tradition and were transcribed two hundred years later, in the thirteenth century. Others believe they were originally composed by a number of anonymous authors. Whether fact or fiction, or a mixture of the two, the Sagas have long been a pillar of Icelandic identity throughout the nation's history—notably during the country's struggle for independence, when they were mobilized for political ends—and continue to be so.

Many individual sagas stand out for their dispassionate portrayals of clan warfare, mythical creatures, betrayal, and justice, though perhaps among the most intriguing are the Vinland Sagas, which describe the first surprise Norse encounter and exploration of the eastern shores by the explorer Leif Erikson of what later came to be known as Canada and the United States of America. (See Chapter 6 for more on Icelandic literature.)

Vinland Sagas: Leif Eriksson Discovers America, by Hans Dahl (1849-1937).

The Icelandic Commonwealth (c. 930-1262)

The medieval Icelandic state was governed by a unique system. The Althing, Iceland's national parliament—and the oldest surviving parliament in the world—was founded in 930 at Þingvellir (Thingvellir), about 28 miles (45 km) northeast of Reykjavik. For two weeks every June, leading chieftains held an assembly to discuss the governance of the land and settle legal disputes. The assemblies were social affairs, attended by free men from all over the country: farmers, traders, craftsmen, storytellers, and, of course, those with grudges to settle. Legal matters were presided over and laws were passed by consensus. By 956 four courts had been established, one for each quarter of the country. The Althing's authority continued for some 330 years, until sovereignty was lost to King Haakon IV of Norway. Iceland remained a Norwegian vassal state until 1380, when the death of the last male in the Norwegian royal bloodline saw Norway, together with its Icelandic dependency, become part of the Kalmar Union, a league of Nordic nations led by Denmark. Later, in the seventeenth century, with the introduction of absolute monarchy, Iceland relinquished its autonomy to the Danish Crown, including the right to legislate. After that, the Althing served almost exclusively as a court of law until 1800, when it was disbanded and a new high court established in Reykjavik in its place.

PAGANISM

As was common in Scandinavia at the time, the early settlers believed in a pantheon of Norse gods and goddesses who were to be venerated, invoked, and appeased through ritual and sacrifice. The Æsir, as the gods were known, lived in the sky kingdom of Asgard, their fortress, which was connected to Midgard, Earth, by a rainbow bridge, the Bifrost. The best-known of the Norse deities include Odin, one-eyed god of sorcery, poetry, and rune craft, who is said to have given his other eye in exchange for wisdom and ridden through the sky on an eight-legged horse; his son Thor, god of thunder and war and defender of Asgard from the gods' adversaries, giants from the celestial land of Jotunheimar; Freyr, god of male fertility; and Loki, god of trickery and deceit. Goddesses were also prominent in early pagan worship. The supreme goddess was Frigg, Odin's wife and the goddess of marriage. Freyja, the sister of Freyr, was the goddess of fertility, beauty, and fine material possessions, and was often invoked during childbirth.

The Arrival of Christianity

Christian missionaries from the British Isles are known to have arrived on the island and operated in the country from the late tenth century onward. A syncretic blend of Christianity and Norse paganism existed for a time, as for example with the early settler Norseman Helgi Magri (939–79), who would invoke Thor when going into battle, but saw no issue in naming his farm Kristnes, Christ Peninsula. As time went on, the divide between adherents of the

Thor, the Norse god of thunder and war, wields his hammer in battle.
Painting by the nineteenth-century artist Mårten Eskil Winge.

old Norse religion and Christianity grew deeper, and by the year 1000 the country was on the brink of civil war. The leaders of the two groups foresaw the dangers of conflict and went to great lengths to avoid it. In the end, Thorgeir Ljosvetningagodi, a pagan chieftain widely respected for his wisdom, was commissioned to find a solution. It is said that he meditated on the matter for three days before announcing his verdict that Iceland should become a Christian country: "If we put asunder the law, we will put asunder the peace. Let it be the foundation of our law that everyone in this country shall be a Christian and believe in one God, Father, Son and Holy Spirit." A number of popular pagan practices, like the eating of horsemeat and the exposure of infants, would still be tolerated for a time.

The Age of Conflict

Iceland has long been a peaceful country. In fact, for more than ten years in a row it has been ranked by the UN as the world's most peaceful country. This was not always the case, however. In the thirteenth century war broke out between the major clans. The country's modest population meant that most of the power was held by only a handful of families, and many of those who fought each other were related. The Age of the Sturlungs, as this period is known, refers to the most powerful clan at the time. The struggle is considered to have begun in 1220, when Snorri Sturluson, an important Icelandic historian, poet, author, and politician of his time, became a vassal of the Norwegian King Haakon IV, who wanted Snorri to help bring Iceland under Norway's rule. Snorri failed in his task, and this was a failure that would later cost him his life. His attempts to introduce the Norwegian monarchy were stiffly opposed by the powerful Sturlung clan and prompted a period of clan warfare that brought the country as close to civil war as it has ever been. Feeling betrayed by what he saw as a lack of effort on Snorri's part, the Norwegian king formed alliances with rival Icelandic chieftains—notably Gissur Thorvaldsson, who later assassinated Snorri in 1241.

The End of Sovereignty

The conflict came to an end only when local clan leaders agreed to accept Norway's sovereignty. In 1262 an agreement, called *Gamli sáttmáli*, or the Old Covenant, was signed by King Haakon IV and the Icelandic chieftains. The signing saw Iceland and Norway form a union, and Snorri's assassin, Gissur, was made Earl of Iceland, the only earl the country has ever had, and a title he held until his death in 1268. According to the agreement, the island's residents would have to pay taxes to their sovereign and be party to its laws. In return Icelandic vessels were granted unfettered trading rights. Furthermore, the King of Norway was now the guarantor of peace on the island. Some would argue that this was the principal reason for the local chieftains' support of the agreement—after decades of civil war and unrest, the clans saw the union with Norway as a chance to end conflict and usher in a new era of peace.

"The English Century" and its Aftermath

In Iceland, the fifteenth century has often been called "the English century." During this time, the English directed a large fleet of commercial and fishing ships to the island in search of new markets. The English merchants brought with them a range of goods that were new to the island, among them textiles, tools, weapons, and wine, and were also able to offer more favorable trading terms than their Norwegian or Danish competitors. The first merchant ship from England is thought to have appeared in the year 1412, and the summer of 1413 saw the arrival of thirty English fishing vessels. There was a rapid increase until a hundred fishing vessels and ten commercial ships were arriving in Iceland from England every year. Iceland had no army (and still hasn't), which meant that the English could act with impunity. In 1425 they arrested the Danish governor over an attempt by the Danish Crown to force an end to the trade, and extradited him to England. In 1467 they killed an Icelandic governor named Bjorn Thorlaksson, who was perceived as an obstacle to

England's trading ambitions. Eventually the English were forced to retreat from the island, owing to a period of protracted armed conflict with Denmark and its ally, Germany, at the turn of the sixteenth century. During the latter half of the century German ships began to sail to Iceland, where they would often compete with the English for trade—competition that would sometimes result in bloody battles. The Danes and their German allies were successful in forcing the British to give up their trade, and, once they had left, the Danes began to rid the island of its German presence too.

The Reformation

The effects of Danish control of the island were far-reaching. The King of Denmark at the time, Christian III, established the Danish Lutheran Church in 1536, and, as territories under Danish sovereignty, Norway, the Faroe Islands, and Iceland were obliged to convert. When fierce protests arose against the authority of the Lutheran Church, the Danish king responded by sending a warship with more than two hundred troops to quell the unrest. A leading Icelandic bishop, Ogmundur Palsson, was arrested and extradited to Denmark, where he later died in custody. It was a great blow to Catholicism on the island. The final blow came when the last Catholic bishop left, Jon Arason, was captured in battle and put to death.

Danish Rule

The seventeenth and eighteenth centuries in Iceland are considered times of considerable hardship. The Danes were now in full control of the country and its administration. Local leaders were forced to swear allegiance to the Danish king, and his governors exercised the power of monarchs. While much of Europe was undergoing

Danish monarch King Christian III.

significant development during this period, the eighteenth century in Iceland was experiencing only worsening misery, with plague, famine, and natural disaster resulting in a substantial decline in population. Air pollution from a massive volcanic eruption at Skaftareldar in 1783 saw approximately 60 percent of the island's livestock wiped out, while the lava spill decimated great swathes of farmland.

The eruption continued for approximately eight months, tearing a seventeen-mile- (27 km-) long fissure on the earth's surface and spewing out around forty-two billion tons of lava. It is estimated that 20 percent of the total population died from the fallout, largely from famine and disease.

Restoration of the Althing

A spirit of romanticism and nationalism seized much of Europe in the nineteenth century, and Iceland was no exception. Local aspirations for national independence began to coalesce, and pressure was mounting on the Danish rulers to relinquish control. As a result a royal decree was issued in 1843, which provided for the reestablishment of Iceland's ancient parliament, the Althing. Elections were held, and in July 1845 the Althing was partially restored as the country's seat of power. For the following three decades the Althing and its twenty-six representatives acted as the local consulting body to the Danish Crown, which retained the final say in all matters pertaining to law and legislation. Then, in 1874, a Constitution was established that saw Iceland receive joint legislative powers with the Crown in all domestic affairs. Executive powers, however, were still held firmly in Danish hands, and Iceland's hopes for full sovereignty remained unfulfilled.

JON SIGURDSSON

Enter Jon Sigurdsson (1811–79), scholar, philologist, editor of the Sagas, and poster boy of the Icelandic independence movement. His struggle for Iceland's independence  was achieved without the firing of a single bullet. Instead, his war was waged in ink and characterized by quiet perseverance. His influence had a big part to play in the restoration of the Althing, Iceland's right to free trade, and devolution of power from the Danish king. Popular during his lifetime, he had a great many supporters from across Icelandic society. When Iceland became a republic in 1944, his birthday, June 17, was declared the country's National Day.

Home Rule and Beyond

A string of developments in the twentieth century paved the way for Iceland's future independence. Home rule was established in 1904, and in 1918 a domestic referendum saw Iceland established as a sovereign kingdom under the Danish Crown. The Icelandic Kingdom now had its own flag and full control of all domestic affairs. As part of the union, however, Iceland would continue to have no military of its own and was obliged to remain neutral in all international conflicts, while Denmark would continue to represent it in all foreign affairs.

The introduction of engine-powered shipping vessels in 1902 jump-started Iceland's industrial revolution and subsequent economic growth. Fish hauls tripled and exports flourished. In 1906 a phone line was established between Iceland and mainland Europe, and in 1911 the country's first university was established in Reykjavik. The capital city expanded at a rapid rate as people began migrating there for work, and by the 1920s, for the first time, there were more people living in a concentrated urban area than in the rest of the country. Hydroelectric power plants that harnessed the power of Iceland's glaciers were constructed, and Reykjavik became electrified, with other larger towns soon to follow suit.

The Birth of the Republic

In sharp contrast to most of Europe, Iceland's experience of the Second World War was not wholly a negative one. On the contrary, it provided the catalyst both for great economic prosperity and for the country's long-awaited political independence. Having declared itself neutral in the conflict, Iceland initially protested against an Allied invasion in 1940 that was aimed at preventing it from falling into German hands. The presence of thousands of British, Canadian, and later American troops, however, ignited Iceland's stagnant economy. (At its peak, there were approximately 30,000 American soldiers stationed on the island—the equivalent of around a quarter of Iceland's entire population at the time.) Jobs were created, and roads and infrastructure were built, including Iceland's only international airport at Keflavik, which had originally served as an American military airbase. The war catapulted the country into a period of sustained economic growth.

The war's political consequences, too, were far-reaching. With Denmark occupied by the Nazis, the Danish Crown's claim to the island was rendered ineffectual. The Icelandic government saw its chance and held a national referendum on the issue of self-rule. The response was unanimous—98 percent of voters supported the motion and finally, on June 17, 1944, full independence was declared.

NATO

Iceland's location took on strategic importance during the postwar years, and its decision to join the North American Treaty Organization was not without controversy. A majority of Iceland's political parties supported membership, but the socialist party did not, and friction between the opposing sides went so far as to turn violent. On one occasion, twelve people were injured in clashes during a protest outside parliament. To begin with, no NATO military force was stationed in the country, but in 1951, following the outbreak of war in Korea, the US and Iceland signed a pact whereby the US accepted full military responsibility for Iceland's defense in exchange for the provision of land for an airbase in Keflavik, in the south of the country. Furthermore, the US committed to providing Iceland with both financial and diplomatic backing. Iceland received a very generous share of the postwar Marshall Plan aid, considering the small size of its population between 1948 and 1951, while it is estimated that up to 5 percent of the country's GDP came from NATO membership during the Cold War. Despite this, the US military presence and NATO membership continued to be matters of domestic controversy. After 1990, as the Cold War came to an end, Iceland's location became far less strategically important, and in 2006 the US pulled out all its military personnel.

Iceland is still a NATO member today, and has been void of any military presence since the US pullout.

The Cod Wars

The Cod Wars were a series of conflicts between Iceland and its NATO ally, the United Kingdom, over the size of the country's national fishing waters. The dispute began in 1958, when Iceland decided to expand its fishing zone from four nautical miles (approx. 7.4 km) to twelve (22 km). This drew protests from all NATO members, while Britain, who saw it as a threat to its lucrative Atlantic resource, responded by announcing that their trawlers would continue to fish there under the armed escort of Royal Navy warships. It was an expensive move for Britain, who needed fifty-three such warships to "protect" its fishing fleet, and highlighted the value those waters held for both countries. The subsequent NATO mediation between the two members saw the Icelandic government threaten to withdraw from NATO entirely, a threat that they would use repeatedly and to great effect. Iceland's withdrawal would mean the end of the US Keflavik military base—a key American strategic foothold in the Arctic region at the time. This leverage over the Americans meant that Britain was forced to back down and accept the limitation on its fishing rights. Iceland played the same hand again in 1972, when it succeeded in increasing its national fishing zone to fifty nautical miles (93 km), and again in 1975 when, realizing the strength of its position, it boldly increased its zone to 200 miles (370 km). Each time the government threatened to pull the country out of NATO if they were not permitted to do so, and the US, acting as mediators, ensured that no such thing would be allowed to take place. With fish exports contributing to a substantial portion of its economy, Iceland was fighting for its economic survival, and the victory over the British remains a point of pride for Icelanders, particularly the older generations.

COVID-19

Despite its isolated and remote location, Iceland was not spared the coronavirus pandemic of 2020, just as it was not able to avoid the great plagues of the Middle Ages, or the deadly outbreak of Spanish Flu brought ashore in 1918. As in much of Europe, the first coronavirus cases were detected on the island in February. From the start, Iceland's approach to tackling the virus consisted of early detection and isolation of infected individuals, social distancing measures, and restrictions on non-essential foreign travel. These measures were largely successful in containing the virus during the first three waves of infection in 2020 and 2021: both the infection and mortality rates were kept low and largely stable throughout. As elsewhere, the greatest fear was that Iceland's health system would find itself overrun in the face of unprecedented pressure—thankfully this was avoided, and the health system proved itself resilient enough to cope.

Daily television briefings were provided by the *þríeyki*—a "trifecta" made up of the country's director of health, chief epidemiologist, and chief superintendent—in order to help keep all citizens abreast of the most important developments. During the first wave of infection in the winter of 2020, universities were closed but elementary and high schools remained open with strict limitations placed upon the number of students permitted in each classroom. The use of masks where distancing measures were not possible was also enforced. A contact-tracing app was launched, though its usage was on a voluntary basis, and measures were put in place to protect users' data and privacy rights. As a result, high penetration was achieved, and close to half the population downloaded and used the app, the highest proportion of any country. In addition, a governmental working group was formed in order to help counter what it called the "information chaos" that proliferated online on social media platforms and elsewhere. In true Icelandic fashion, its existence was criticized by politicians and media pundits alike, who feared that it would open the door to government censorship. Unsurprisingly to some, those fears were not realized.

In June and July 2020, Iceland reopened its borders to non-essential visitors from more than forty countries. Though visitor numbers remained low (70 to 80 percent lower than in the summer of 2019), it provided a much-needed lifeline to the country's tourism sector—one of the central pillars of the Icelandic economy.

GOVERNMENT AND POLITICS

As they were the last European nation to achieve full independence, the Icelanders don't take their political obligations for granted. This is most tangible around election time, when public debate on the current economic and political issues can often become heated.

Iceland is a constitutional republic and operates a multiparty system based on proportional representation. The legislative arm, the Althing, is made up of sixty-three elected parliamentarians who are voted in every four years. There is an independent judiciary, with both a supreme court and district courts. The political landscape is broadly similar to that of other Nordic countries, with a social democratic party, a liberal pro-free-market party, a socialist party, and a "center" party. Despite the modest size of the population, political consensus remains elusive: no party has ever achieved an

The modern Althing, Iceland's seat of government, Reykjavik.

absolute majority in elections, and the government is always made up of a coalition of two or more parties. Party loyalty, once considered important, is no longer adhered to, and there is far greater fluidity between parties among younger voters.

As elsewhere in Europe, Iceland's traditional parties have seen their monopolies dissipate due to the formation of new, smaller contenders, which have come about either as the result of intra-party conflict, or because a single issue has become so polarizing as to prompt the formation of an entirely new party, as for example with the country's fishing quota. Few of the new contending parties survive for more than a term or two, and the politicians will either reunite with their home party or seek new employment. The following is a basic breakdown of four main political parties.

The Independence Party
Formed in 1929, this has traditionally been Iceland's biggest party. It supports free market capitalism and liberal conservatism, and is Eurosceptic. At its strongest in the first decades of independence, the party's influence in recent years has waned.

The Social Democratic Alliance
Formed to unite the fractured left-wing parties against the ruling Independence Party in 1999, the Social Democratic Alliance supports economic and social intervention such as progressive taxation and a broad welfare state in line with a social democratic outlook. It is the only major party to support EU membership. Support for the party has shrunk in recent elections.

The Left-Green Movement
This movement was founded in 1999 by members of the Althing who did not approve of the formation of the umbrella left-wing Social Democratic Alliance. Its stance was formed mainly in opposition to the direction taken by the SDA's pro-European agenda. Today, the movement supports pacifism, democratic socialism, environmentalism, and feminism, and opposes EU membership.

The Progressive Party
Also known as The Farmers' Party, this centrist-

libertarian party was founded in 1916 to represent the agricultural sector and to fight for the interests of rural communities. Though never popular enough to garner a large percentage of votes, it has often found a place in both left- and right-wing government coalitions.

The President

Iceland's president is the head of state, and is voted for in national elections every four years. Although the second article of the Constitution states that legislative powers are shared by parliament and the president, the presidential office has largely been limited to signing bills passed by parliament. In fact, the office's ability to veto a bill has only ever been exercised by one president out of six: Olaf Ragnar Grimsson, who held office for five consecutive terms from 1996 to 2016, vetoed parliamentary legislation on three separate occasions.

Vigdis Finnbogadottir, Iceland's president from 1980 to 1996.

ICELAND'S FIRST FEMALE HEAD OF STATE

Vigdis Finnbogadottir became Iceland's first female president in 1980 after defeating three male opponents with 33.3 percent of the vote. A divorcée and a single mother, Finnbogadottir was a political newcomer—she had previously been the director of the Reykjavik Theater Company, and a French teacher on Iceland's state television channel. Finnbogadottir proved a highly capable and popular head of state who went on to win reelection a further three times. Her presidency of sixteen years makes her the longest-running elected female head of state in the world. Her motto is: "Never let the women down."

The Question of EU Membership

Icelandic attitudes to EU membership are complex. The majority of political parties are opposed to joining the Union, the Social Democratic Alliance being the only exception. The party decided to apply for membership of the EU when it held the reins during the 2008 financial crisis, a move that, along with perceived economic mismanagement, saw the government thrown out at the next election and the application swiftly withdrawn.

Despite not being a member, Iceland is heavily integrated into the Union by way of the European Economic Area agreement (the EEA) of 1992, which included it in the European single market. As Iceland exports most of its goods and services to other EU countries, joining the EEA was of paramount importance. It also means that Icelandic citizens have freedom of movement within the Union, and have full rights to live, work, set up businesses, invest, and buy homes in any EU countries, and gives the same rights to EU citizens in Iceland.

Supporters of full EU membership point out that the EEA's common rules are constantly updated by new legislation; however, because Iceland is not a full EU member, it does not have the capacity to affect this legislation, though it is obliged to adhere to it. Those who support the current state of affairs point out that if Iceland were to join the EU, it would have to adhere to a whole host of extra rules and regulations that might not be suitable for its needs, for example rules regarding fishing and fishing quotas.

Hrunid: The Crash

Ask any Icelander where they were on October 6, 2008, and they will be able to tell you. This was the day when Iceland stood on the brink of economic collapse, when the then prime minister Geir Haarde warned the country of imminent national bankruptcy in what was later dubbed his "God bless Iceland" speech. It was approximately two months after the fall of the American investment bank Lehman Brothers, the fallout of which sent shock waves throughout the global economy. All but one of Iceland's banks had collapsed as a result. The potential consequence of their collapse can be appreciated only when one takes into account that by 2007, following a lucrative decade of privatization and liberalization of the financial sector, the assets of the country's banks stood at ten times the value of the country's entire GDP. While in many other countries the banks were reluctantly bailed out, in Iceland their sheer size meant that they were simply too big to save and so were allowed to fail, lest the rest of the country, as Haarde put it, "be sucked into the whirlpool with them."

Iceland weathered the storm comparatively well, and the economy was helped by a combination of factors. The government guaranteed all domestic deposits, and the steep depreciation of Iceland's currency, the krona, meant that the country's vital export market was given a much-needed boost, and a healthy trade balance surplus was achieved.

The economy's narrow escape from complete collapse did little to quell public anger, the primary targets of which were the bankers. As the result of a parliamentary investigation, a total of thirty-six

individuals, the majority of them bankers, received
jail sentences for their parts in the crash. Hreidar Mar
Sigurdsson, the former director of what had been
one of the country's largest banks, Kaupthing Bank,
received a five-and-a-half-year jail sentence for his
part, the heaviest sentence of all. Nor was the political
class spared the public's ire—widespread protest
over what was perceived as careless mismanagement
saw the government resign in January 2009 and a
temporary government appointed until elections were
held later that year.

Misfortune Shared

A popular joke at the time: "What is the
difference between Iceland and Ireland?" "One
letter and six months," referring to the recent
economic troubles of their Irish neighbors.

Post-Crash Politics

Having proved itself to be an effective and powerful
force during the years of post-crash recovery, public
sentiment has continued to be instrumental in
Icelandic politics. In 2016, prime minister Sigmundur
David Gunnlaugsson was forced to resign following
the release of the Panama Papers, a journalistic
investigation that exposed the widespread use of tax

havens by government figures around the world. Leaked documents showed that his wife had owned an offshore company with links to some of Iceland's collapsed banks.

The following coalition government collapsed in less than a year due to public pressure after a scandal in which the prime minister's father wrote a letter recommending that a convicted pedophile should have his name cleared.

THE ECONOMY

Iceland's economy is a blend of free-market capitalism, government intervention, and a strong welfare state. Centuries of eking out a living at the mercy of nature's forces has ensured that opportunities, when they do arise, are not wasted. This *vertíðarhugarfar*, or "fishing-season mentality," (see page 54) means that the net will be cast again and again to make the most of what is available today—perhaps even until there are no fish left, as was very nearly the case by the 1980s when fish stocks, Iceland's life blood, were on the verge of collapse. Today they are protected and flourishing.

The difficult balance between prosperity and ecological responsibility is one that Icelanders know intimately, whether in harnessing the raw power of its waterways to enable the production of energy-hungry aluminum, or the pursuit of a seemingly unlimited number of tourists at the expense of the natural integrity of certain sites.

The economy witnessed a remarkable recovery following the crash of 2008, helped in large part by the country's tourism industry. Today Iceland has a GDP per capita of over US $60,000, placing it in the global top 5 percent. Living costs are high, and the working week is among the longest in Europe, though many would say these downsides are comfortably offset by local salary rates and high living standards. Prior to the coronavirus pandemic in 2020, the country's current account was in surplus, growth was strong, and unemployment was under 3 percent. At the time of writing, the long-term effects of the pandemic on Iceland's economy have yet to become clear.

Tourism

Prior to 2020, tourism was the largest sector of Iceland's export-based economy, and accounted for approximately 10 percent of the country's total GDP. At its height it employed some 14 percent of the country's entire workforce, and the country's popularity as a travel destination played a central role in its economic recovery following the crash. Despite the relatively high cost of travel within the country, the number of foreign visitors arriving to Iceland each year continued to grow—between 2008 and 2018 visitor numbers increased by a total of 380 percent. The unabated growth in the number of tourists had put a considerable strain on the industry's resources and there were those, both locals and visitors, who felt that certain tourist hotspots had surpassed their level of capacity and were at risk of becoming irrevocably damaged. A number of local campaigns were launched calling for action to be taken to preserve these sites. A variety of solutions were proposed in response, including the dispersal of flight arrivals through two additional airports located in other parts of the country, in order to reduce the load on the popular southern region. Others went as far as to suggest a curb on the number of visitors during the busy summer season.

While the coronavirus pandemic put an almost total stop to Iceland's tourism industry in 2020 and much of 2021, it is expected that things will return to normality in due course, though it remains to be seen how quickly the bounce-back will materialize, and to what extent tourism will regain its position as the central pillar of Iceland's economy. That said, the lull has presented something of an opportunity; when tourism does get going again the industry has been given a chance to ensure that things are pursued in a more sustainable fashion and so safeguard itself and its main sites for generations to come.

Icelandic fishermen in Reykjavik process the day's catch.

Fishing

Iceland is among the world's top twenty fishing
nations, despite having one of the smallest populations
of any country. Fisheries and their related industries
are an integral part of the country's economy,
constituting approximately 40 percent of exports and
employing nearly 10 percent of the workforce. As
previously mentioned, the industry has long struggled
with balancing sustainable fishing practices with
profitability. Overfishing of certain species such as
herring and cod in the 1960s and '70s led to a drastic
decline in fish stocks and, as a result, the government
introduced a quota system that gives each boat owner

the right to catch a limited proportion of the total permitted catch for each species of fish. The approach has been successful and today none of Iceland's harvested species are considered at risk of overfishing.

Industry

Benefiting from an abundance of cheap energy harnessed from natural waterways and geothermal heat, Iceland has emerged as a world-leading producer of aluminum and silicone, both of which require huge amounts of energy to produce. Aluminum production alone accounts for 25 percent of the country's exports and earns some US $2bn annually. The impact of hydroelectric projects on glacial rivers and the environment has been a point of contention for locals, who are wary of damaging the country's natural beauty with the construction of dams and industrial plants.

CHAPTER TWO

VALUES & ATTITUDES

Generalizing about nations and their cultural traits will take one only so far, and, of course, is not without its risks. However, common attitudes in Iceland certainly exist, and it's helpful to be aware of them, particularly for those visitors who would like to form friendships that are based on mutual understanding with their Icelandic hosts.

THETTA REDDAST: "IT'LL BE OK"

One extremely popular attitude is succinctly summed up by the Icelandic phrase *þetta reddast*—pronounced "thetta reddast"—which is used to express the firmly held belief that everything will turn out all right in the end, that it will be so without the need for extensive planning or worry, and that one should be ready to

adapt to the circumstances, whatever they require.
While a Norwegian, Dane, or Swede may be more
inclined to engage in meticulous organizing, the
Icelander is more sensitive to the unpredictability of
life, so flexibility and a basic optimism that things
will turn out for the best are more highly valued. And
how could it be otherwise? Iceland is not stable—it
is perched on the convergence of two tectonic plates
and has more than thirty volcanoes that could erupt
at any time. The weather can change dramatically,
and the country's economic health is almost entirely
determined by the price of aluminum, fish, and the
number of tourists who decide to visit in the year—
factors that are largely out of anyone's control, as the
coronavirus pandemic has once again made clear. It
was only a couple of generations ago that the majority
of Icelanders were farmers and fisherman who were at
the mercy of nature and extreme weather conditions,
and so, having become highly attuned to uncertainty
and the necessity of adaptation, they have developed
a more flexible and optimistic attitude toward life and
its twists and turns.

STUBBORN SELF-RELIANCE

Iceland's Nobel laureate, Halldor Laxness, tells us
much about the importance of self-reliance and self-

sufficiency as ideals in Icelandic society in his epic novel *Independent People*. The story's protagonist, Bjartur, is a farmhand who toils for eighteen years for his freedom, after which he faces a constant struggle to survive as a free man in the inhospitable environment of the remote highlands—and it comes at a heavy price. Bjartur loses two wives and seven children in the process, and yet he is not

Iceland's Nobel laureate Halldor Laxness, 1955.

deflected. His stubbornness, his will to persevere along his path, so long as it is his own, even to the detriment of himself and those around him, is a trait with which many on the island can identify. Anti-authoritarianism in Iceland goes back a long way—all the way, in fact, to the first Norse settlers who arrived on the island after fleeing subjugation in Norway.

While it took Iceland many centuries to achieve national self-rule, the ideal of self-sufficiency on both a national and an individual level never lost its significance, and is still very much in evidence today. It explains the lack of pomp and formality the Icelanders grant their politicians, because, of course, they could do just as well without them. It also explains why Icelanders are not the best at accepting criticism. The unheeded warnings of foreign analysts and economic observers prior to the crash of 2008 are an important example of this: "How could an outsider know what the Icelandic economy needs better than we do?" It explains why Icelandic teenagers set themselves up to work from such a young age, and why an Icelander will always own his or her home when given the chance. (For more on industrious teenagers and the importance of private property, see Chapter 5.)

Iceland's dependence on its neighbors, distant though they may be, is not easily overlooked. However, if Laxness's novel tells us anything about modern Icelanders, it may be that, though independence and dogged stubbornness come at a price, it is a price that they are, more often than not, willing to pay.

"FISHING-SEASON MENTALITY": CATCH THEM WHILE YOU CAN

As any fisherman will tell you, when the season is right and the shoal appears, the time has come to cast your net. And, more than that, cast as many nets as you can, because tomorrow may already be too late. The Icelanders have a word for this—*vertíðarhugarfar*—which can be translated roughly as "fishing-season mentality." It describes the almost gung-ho manner in which people will make the most of an opportunity that presents itself, to the extent that they may sometimes end up going too far and, in doing so, damage their own prospects of continued success.

Until the Second World War, Iceland was among the poorest countries in Europe. Though marine engineering had revolutionized the fishing industry and increased the ability to catch and export fish, the Great Depression of the First World War brought the local economy to its knees. The arrival of foreign troops in Iceland as part of the Allied occupation (at one point this numbered more than half the entire male population of the country) meant that the war became something of a gift from above, and explains why some on the island remember it as the *blessað stríðið*, "the blessed war."

The boost provided by the extra money in the economy as a result of the influx of Allied troops, as well as of the investment in infrastructure, rapidly turned the country's fortunes around. Some say the speed at which progress came was too fast for Iceland to handle, and that its good fortune went to its head. There was rapid investment in shipping and fisheries. As mentioned in the previous chapter, over-intensive fishing practices, with little regard for the sustainability of fish stocks and the wider social implications of their depletion, meant that by the

1960s and '70s, Iceland had simply exhausted most of its herring and cod stocks, the fallout of which was still felt decades later.

Many saw parallels in the rapid expansion of Iceland's tourism sector. To put things in perspective, Iceland's population was matched by visitors for the first time in the year 2000, with 300,000 tourists. This number rose to 500,000 in 2010. The next decade, however, saw the figure balloon to over 2.5 million. Prior to the coronavirus pandemic, the strain, and in some cases damage, caused to the country's most popular natural sites and trails prompted fears that history was repeating itself and that the industry was jeopardizing its future success by pursuing unlimited growth. New hotels continue to be built despite a general economic slowdown: might they one day be left standing empty as testament to Iceland's *vertíðarhugarfar*?

GENDER EQUALITY

Icelanders take gender equality seriously, and their efforts have yielded impressive results: Iceland has topped the World Economic Forum's gender equality table for seven years running. As President Gudni Johannesson points out, a nation with a population of 350,000 simply cannot afford to have half of its population outside the workforce. Today, more than

80 percent of working-age women are in employment. In January 2018, Iceland became the first country to make it a crime to pay men more than women for the same job, and companies with more than twenty-five employees must obtain government verification that levels of pay meet standards of equality. Women make up 66 percent of university graduates, and hold approximately half of the country's sixty parliamentary seats. State-subsidized childcare is a right, and parents have a total of nine months' maternity and paternity leave, during which time they receive 80 percent of their salaries. Fathers and mothers each receive three months' leave, and the remaining three months may be split as the couple wishes. (See Chapter 8 for more on gender equality in the workplace.)

MARRIAGE AND MORES

Public attitudes toward marriage and family in Iceland are relaxed. To most Icelanders, it is simply none of their concern who you live with or how you conduct your private life. The family unit is still important, and the norm, but for many the institution of marriage is far less so. So much so, in fact, that in 2018 more than 70 percent of children in Iceland were born to parents out of wedlock—the highest of any country in the world. The fertility rate among Icelandic women is also in steady decline and is now at its lowest on record, at approximately 1.7 children per woman. Those women who choose to have children are also opting to have them later in life—twenty-eight is now the average age for first-time mothers, a substantial shift from just a generation ago, when most women would have had their first baby before the age of twenty-one. At the turn of the millennium, about three-quarters of couples marrying opted for a religious ceremony, whereas today that figure has come down to about half. (For more on marriage and the family in Iceland, see Chapter 5.)

GAY ICELAND

Iceland is proud of its progressive stance on sexuality. Laws that criminalized homosexual activity were abolished in 1942, and, although there's still some way to go toward complete equality, Iceland is a comfortable and accepting place to be gay, where the rights to marriage, children, and protection against discrimination are enshrined in law. A recent study by the Organization for Economic Co-operation and Development found Iceland to be the least homophobic of any OECD country. Widespread acceptance, however, was not earned without its share of struggle. In 1975, when the well-known local singer and stage producer Hordur Torfason went public with his sexuality in an

Participants at Reykjavik's popular Pride Parade, 2019.

interview in the men's magazine *Samúel* the level of
vitriol he faced was crushing. He became the victim
of both verbal and physical abuse, and soon found
himself unable to find work or rent an apartment,
eventually fleeing to Denmark. It was only after
coming close to taking his own life in his apartment
in Copenhagen that he decided to fight the injustice
that he and others like him faced. Change did not
come overnight, but the effect of his visibility and
pride on public debate was powerful. The formation
of Samtökin '78, an organization set up by Hordur to
fight for gay rights, marked a milestone and saw the
movement gain in both members and supporters.

Civil partnership for same-sex couples was
eventually introduced in 1996, later replaced with a
gender-neutral marriage law in 2010. In 2006 same-
sex couples won the right to adopt children, and IVF
insemination treatment too became available. In
2015 the Church of Iceland voted to allow same-sex
couples to marry in its churches, and Article 65 of the
Constitution prohibits discrimination against anyone
based on their sexual orientation.

The Reykjavik Pride festival is celebrated annually
in August, and attracts tens of thousands of people
from all over the world. The event has come a long
way since its inception in 1999, when there were
perhaps 1,500 onlookers. Today it is a colorful six-day
celebration that hosts a wide range of events.

THE WORLD'S FIRST OPENLY LESBIAN HEAD OF GOVERNMENT

The struggle for gay rights and wider social acceptance has come a long way in Iceland. Today, there are a number of well-known and publicly celebrated LGBTQ Icelanders who have succeeded in their fields. Among them is Johanna Sigurdardottir, a labor union activist who went on to become the world's first openly gay head of government during one of Iceland's most turbulent periods. Having held a number of ministerial portfolios for the ruling Social Democratic party after entering politics in the 1970s, she was appointed interim prime minister when the head of government resigned in 2009 in the face of public anger over the financial crisis that threatened the country. Public acceptance of Johanna Sigurdardottir's leadership was proved when she won the national elections later that year. During her term same-sex marriage was legalized, and in 2010 she married her long-term partner, novelist Jonina Leosdottir.

NATIONALISM

The Icelanders are proud of their country, their artists, their ancient Sagas, their peaceful struggle for independence, and, more recently, their football team. However, it is a quiet pride, and one you will not often hear discussed. If you see flags being paraded in public, they are far more likely to be celebrating a sporting event than for any political cause. National pride and national consciousness were important driving forces on the country's long road to national independence in 1944; however, since achieving its goal the national movement has all but disappeared. Since independence, far-right political groups have only ever played an extremely minor role. At its peak,

A woman celebrates Iceland's UEFA Euro 2016 performance. In Iceland, sporting events are one of the few occasions where you will see public displays of national pride.

the short-lived Icelandic fascist party of the 1930s and
'40s won 2.8 percent of the vote in Reykjavik's local
elections. The introduction of an Icelandic National
Front in the 2016 elections resulted in even poorer
results—they received just 0.16 percent of the votes in
two constituencies. Some say nationalistic sentiment
is on the rise in modern Iceland following an influx
of foreign workers, but there is no statistical data or
evidence to back this up.

A HELPING HAND

Being there for your neighbor in time of need is a
duty that all Icelanders are ready to fulfill. Historical
reasons for people's readiness to help in Iceland are
not hard to find. Since the time of the first settlers, the
island's harsh environment has meant that relations
with your neighbor could mean the difference
between life and death. Reciprocal support of one's
immediate neighbors and wider community have
long provided a safety net on both an individual and a
societal level. Take, for example, Iceland's Search and
Rescue teams. Made up entirely of volunteers, these
highly trained units are ready to respond to all manner
of natural and man-made emergencies; whether you
have been caught in an avalanche or a snow storm,
have been swept away at sea, fallen down a crevasse,

Search and Rescue volunteers help to free a car stranded in deep snow in Jökuldalsheiði, eastern Iceland.

or become lost in the freezing wilderness, there are a hundred national teams, made up of 4,000 volunteers on constant standby to provide assistance. A further 10,000 volunteers make up the organization's extensive manpower resources. These well-respected units are funded entirely by donations. In a country with such a hostile environment, no army, and a limited police force, communal support is not a luxury but a necessity.

Similar values are also observable on a broader societal level. The Icelanders are extremely proud of their universal health care and high-quality education from nursery to university. For a country of only 300,000 people, this is no easy feat, and it took some time to build a system where all are afforded basic rights in health and education. A state pension also ensures that anyone over the age of sixty-seven will have a basic level of income to support them.

A PAGAN RENAISSANCE

Though more than 60 percent of Icelanders belong to the Lutheran Church, attendance of religious services such as at Christmas or on Sundays is low—and dropping further still. For many in Iceland today, membership of the Church is maintained largely out of habit, but little else. It is not necessarily that Icelanders do not feel a need for spirituality; it is more that a growing number do not believe that such a need is met by the Church.

Enter Iceland's oldest, and now fastest-growing religion: Ásatrú, the old Norse paganism of the island's original Viking settlers. The dominant religion in Iceland before the country's Christianization in 1000, it was finally re-recognized by the state in 1973 and is today the largest non-Christian religion on the island. But what is Ásatrú today, and why, despite the fact that it doesn't engage in proselytizing or missionary work, are more and more people drawn to it every year? Well, for starters, there is no prescribed dogma, no code of religious laws, and no formalized prayer. This alone is bound to hold an appeal for many Icelanders, knowing as we do how they feel about authority.

According to Hilmar Örn Hilmarsson, the current high priest of Ásatrúarfélagið (Iceland's largest heathen group), Ásatrú is a religion of "peace and respect," and one that "teaches you how to live in harmony with your surroundings and yourself, and how to deal with the different phases of your life." Though there is no official theological stance, a pantheistic world view—one that believes in the divine nature of all natural phenomena—is often espoused, and the movement's emphasis on the natural environment and ecological health is certainly part of its appeal today. As former Ásatrú leader Jónína K. Berg put it, "Ásatrú is a pantheistic belief. The earth, the air and the water has great value to us. We are a part of the earth and not its masters." The socially progressive and political stances of Ásatrúarfélagið too have been instrumental: among other things, Ásatrú supports LGBT rights and same-sex marriage, as well as the separation of Church and State.

With no clearly identifiable theology or praxis to speak of, it is the yearly rituals, or *blót*, that unify the community in Iceland today. Originally, *blót* consisted of blood sacrifices, but the Ásatrú of today rejects animal sacrifice. Instead, festivities typically involve the symbolic use of ritualistic objects, such as animal horns, reciting Norse poetry, playing music, offering libations to the gods, and of course, a hearty feast. The four main *blót* today include Jólablót, held on the

Ásatrú High Priest Jörmundur Ingi Hansen at Þingvellir.

winter solstice, Sigurblót on the first day of summer, Sumarblót on the summer solstice, and Veturnáttablót on the first day of winter. Ásatrú priests today also perform important life cycle rituals, such as naming ceremonies, coming-of-age ceremonies, marriages, including same-sex marriages, and funerals, providing an alternative to those who seek to give meaning to important life cycle events but who do not feel at home in the Church.

CHAPTER THREE

CUSTOMS &
TRADITIONS

Iceland hasn't always used the Gregorian calendar. Until the eighteenth century it operated according to a lunar calendar that divided the year into months of "short days" and "nightless days," corresponding roughly to winter and summer, and individual months and festivals were tied to the cycle of seasons. For example, the weeks that fall between mid-December and mid-January were called Mörsugur, "fat-sucking month," and mid-July to mid-August was called Heyannir, "hay business month." Though the traditional calendar is no longer in use, some of the old festivals and feast days are still celebrated.

Iceland's main festivals largely follow those of other Western countries, with some notable exceptions, among them modern renditions of old pagan holy days that predate the arrival of Christianity in Iceland.

FESTIVALS AND HOLIDAYS

Thorrablot

Today a popular midwinter party, Thorrablot (Þorrablót) was once a festival of sacrifice to Iceland's pagan Norse gods. The festival, which falls on the first Friday after January 19, was abolished during the Christianization of the country around the eleventh century, but reemerged in the second part of the nineteenth century with the advent of romantic nationalism that looked to the country's ancient rites for inspiration. Thorrablot went mainstream in the 1960s, when a Reykjavik eatery began serving forgotten local delicacies such as fermented shark, congealed sheep's blood wrapped in a ram's stomach, ram testicles boiled and cured in lactic acid, singed and boiled sheep's heads, dried fish, and sour whale blubber. Nowadays Thorrablot is an occasion for friends and family to gather during the darkest and coldest months, to eat, drink, and have a good time together. Organizations and offices also plan Thorrablot parties for their employees. The drink of choice, Brennivin—also known as "black death"—is an unsweetened schnapps made from potatoes and caraway. The level of alcohol is 40 percent, so do take it slowly if you decide to use it to wash down the whale blubber.

Valentine's Day

While many older Icelanders may shake their heads
at the mention of Valentine's Day, it has become
popular to express affection to your significant other
on February 14. Restaurants fill up with bookings, and
couples exchange small gifts, as is common in other
countries. For those looking for a more traditional
way to express their love, Iceland's lunar calendar
assigned the first day of the month of Thorri (Þorri),
which usually starts in mid-January, as Husband's Day,
when lucky men around the country are pampered by
their wives. Husbands have a chance to convey their
devotion on the first day of the following month, Góa,
which is Wife's Day. Both are still celebrated today
with gifts and a general lavishing of attention.

Easter

Easter in Iceland is a five-day holiday celebrated by all,
regardless of religious affiliation. The festival begins
on Maundy Thursday, a public holiday on which
shops and public institutions close. Some restaurants
remain open, but it is wise to stock up on supplies
beforehand. Good Friday is traditionally a day of
solemn contemplation, and in Iceland festivities on
this day were until recently illegal. In typical anti-
authoritarian style, groups of Icelanders would protest
the law every year by gathering to play a large public
game of bingo, though no one was ever arrested. Today,

there are no restrictions on cultural events such as theater performances and art exhibitions. Traditions over the Easter weekend include an Easter egg hunt and a traditional lamb dinner on Sunday night. Monday is another day of rest, relaxation, and family time. Churches will hold Easter services and, if you are in Reykjavik, the church of Hallgrímskirkja, close to the city center, normally hosts a program of interesting concerts that can be well worth attending. Many Icelanders use the five-day break to do some traveling, with skiing being a popular option.

The First Day of Summer

The first Thursday after April 18 is a public holiday that celebrates the start of the summer season according to the traditional lunar calendar. Though the highest recorded temperature on this day is only 56.3°F (13.5 °C), and it has even been known to snow, it is nonetheless a celebration of the end of the dark winter and the lengthening of days. Towns around the country mark the occasion with parades and organize public events for all to enjoy—just don't forget to wrap up well!

National Day

June 17 marks Iceland's National Day. Full independence was declared on this day in 1944, and was chosen for being the birthday of Jon Sigursson,

College graduates take part in National Day celebrations in Akureyri, Iceland's capital of the north.

that key figure of the Icelandic independence movement in the nineteenth century. The day is celebrated in Reykjavik and all major towns with concerts, parades, public performances, and activities for children. It is also one of the few times of year that Icelandic national dress (Þjóðbúningurinn) makes a public appearance.

Midsummer's Night

Summer time in Iceland is a unique experience. From mid-May onward darkness is nowhere to be found, and the sun remains visible for twenty-four hours a day. The season of the Midnight Sun reaches its peak, the summer solstice, on approximately June 21, after which the days begin to shorten. Midsummer Night is celebrated on June 24. Locally named Jonmessa, the day commemorates the birthday of John the Baptist, though little religious association remains today. Rather, the day is awash with superstition; it is said that cows gain the ability to speak, that seals take human form, and that rolling around naked in the dew at midnight can heal the sick. The day is not a public holiday, and in general bonfires are not lit as they are in neighboring Scandinavian countries; however, there is a tradition of going on a long solstice walk.

Merchant's Bank Holiday

Few national holidays in Iceland are celebrated with as much intensity as Merchant's Bank Holiday. It is a three-day public holiday on the first weekend of August, and is accompanied by an exodus of people from the capital region who make the most of the summer break by traveling around the country. Many towns hold music festivals, art exhibitions and installations, and activities for families. Some of the larger festivals, such as those in Akureyri or Reykjavik, require tickets and can get pretty lively, with thousands of partygoers attending. The biggest festival is probably Thjodhatid (Þjóðhátíð), The National Festival, on the Westman Islands, which draws some 18,000 visitors. The weekend used to have a reputation for drink, drugs, and general debauchery, particularly for teenagers. Newspaper headlines highlighting the rowdy behavior would regularly follow, and it became a concern for authorities. Today, however, things have been cleaned up quite a bit, and the weekend no longer keeps worried parents awake at night.

Christmas

December in Iceland is a very dark month indeed. However, the snow, the festive decorations, and the opportunity to see the Northern Lights spread across the night sky make it a very special time of year. Christmas in Iceland officially begins on December 24, but the festivities traditionally begin on December 11. On that day most families put up their Christmas

Jólakötturinn, Iceland's legendary Christmas Cat, is rumored to have an appetite for children who do not wear new clothes on Christmas Eve.

Statues of Grýla and Leppalúði, the ghoulish parents of Iceland's Yule Lads, in Akureyri. Naughty children beware!

trees, and at nightfall children leave their shoes by the window for Iceland's mythical Christmas pranksters, the Yule Lads, to fill them up with sweets or a small gift (naughty children might get a potato!). There are thirteen Yule Lads, with names such as Door-Slammer and Spoon-Licker, who come to town, one a night, to harass the inhabitants—or so the tale goes. Iceland's original December festival predates the arrival of Christianity. Historically held on December 21, the shortest, darkest day of the year, the pagan Yule marked the lengthening of days following the winter solstice when there are only four hours of daylight. Today, as elsewhere, the celebration of Christmas centers on the family, and a festive spirit prevails well into January.

Mass of Thorlak

The Mass of Saint Thorlak, the Patron Saint of Iceland, is held on December 23. On this day most families will clean their houses thoroughly and eat a traditional meal of extremely strong-smelling, ammonia-fermented skate fish, often with potatoes. This is also a big shopping day, on which people rush to pick up last-minute gifts. For this reason, many shops stay open as late as midnight.

Christmas Eve (Jól Eve, Aðfangadagur)

In Iceland the main Christmas meal is eaten on Christmas Eve. Shops close early and restaurants book up weeks in advance, so forward planning is advised. Family and friends come together in the evening to enjoy the Christmas meal, which traditionally consists of smoked lamb with vegetables. After the meal, presents are exchanged and opened, and some people continue on to Midnight Mass.

Christmas Day (Jól Day, Jóladagur)

The day is usually spent relaxing, eating, and enjoying the festive spirit with extended family and friends. Lunch is the main meal of the day and will traditionally consist of a roast leg of lamb or a game bird. Another traditional Christmas Day food is a very thin, crisp

Decorating leaf bread, Iceland's traditional Christmas Day treat.

flatbread called leaf bread (*laufabrauð*), which looks rather like a snowflake. It is often made at home, with all the family taking part in decorating the bread; some families have their own particular pattern that they use for this.

The Last Day of Christmas
January 6 is the last day of Christmas in Iceland, and is known locally as the thirteenth day of Christmas. Large family meals are held and bonfires lit as people bid farewell to Christmas. The night is considered to have a supernatural quality; it is on this night that trolls and elves move houses, that seals take on human form, and that cows once more gain the ability to speak (though, unlike on the summer solstice, only for one hour). It also marks the departure of the last

Yule Lad, Candle-Beggar, who was known to follow children around in order to steal their candles (once made from tallow and edible) in order to eat them. He is, incidentally, also the most popular Yule Lad among Icelanders, so at least he has that going for him, even if candles are no longer edible.

New Year's Eve

New Year's Eve in Iceland starts with a festive meal held for family and friends at about 6:00 p.m. After the meal, many people congregate around local bonfires with friends and neighbors. Once the bonfires are over, by about 9:00 p.m., the streets empty as everyone heads home to watch the nation's annual New Year's

A New Year's bonfire, Reykjavik.

television comedy show, "Aramotaskaup." Largely satire, the show pokes fun at politicians and other public figures and, with English subtitles, visitors to Iceland can join the other 90 percent of the population in watching it. As midnight approaches, people take to the streets for hours of fireworks and general merriment. While some will head home again, many go on to house parties and bars to continue the celebrations into the early hours.

PUBLIC HOLIDAYS

New Year's Day January 1

Maundy Thursday The Thursday before Easter

Easter Usually in April. Includes Good Friday, Easter Sunday, and Easter Monday

First Day of Summer On a Thursday between April 19 and 25

Labor Day May 1

Ascension Day On a Thursday, forty days after Easter Sunday

Whit Sunday Ten days after Ascension Day

Whit Monday The day after Whit Sunday

National Day June 17

Bank Holiday Monday The first Monday in August

Christmas Eve December 24

Christmas Day December 25

Boxing Day December 26

New Year's Eve December 31

LIFE CYCLE EVENTS

As previously discussed, though Iceland is very much a secular country today, more than 60 percent of the population still belong to the Evangelical Lutheran Church. As such, the Church often provides the framework for important life cycle events, even if those partaking do not necessarily identify with the religious undertones of these occasions.

Baptisms and Naming Ceremonies

Baptism most commonly takes place a month after the baby is born, and is the occasion on which the parents reveal the child's name. This is a joyous affair, and is usually followed by a baptismal feast with family and friends. Today, however, more and more parents are opting to hold a secular "naming party" in place of a traditional baptism.

Uniquely, it is a legal requirement that names in Iceland are selected from a database of names approved by the Icelandic Naming Committee, established in 1991. Its job is to ensure that the use of traditional Icelandic names continues, and to prevent the introduction of new, non-Icelandic names. If parents want to choose a name that is not on the list, they must submit it to the committee for approval. Names must use the Icelandic alphabet, fit the language's grammatical structure, and be proven to have some traditional Icelandic precedent. The naming system is not without controversy, however. As more people from other countries have taken up residence on the island in recent years, debate has intensified, with many calling for the restrictions to be lifted. Despite numerous attempts by parliamentarians to have the committee abolished, the regulations remain in place.

In Iceland today, popular names for women include Guðrún, Anna, and Kristín, while for men Jón, Sigurður, and Guðmundur are the most common. Family names in Iceland are not usually used. Rather, last names most often take the first name of the father, with the suffix *son* or *dóttir* added for a son or a daughter. So, for example, Sigurður's daughter may be called Kristín Sigurðurdottir.

Confirmation

Confirmation, a ceremony to strengthen and deepen one's connection to God and the Christian faith, serves to confirm the baptism. Traditionally, all children who are baptized undergo a confirmation ceremony at the age of fourteen, usually after undergoing instruction in the traditions and beliefs of the Church. It is a happy occasion for families, usually followed by a family party, when the young person receives presents from those attending.

A secular alternative is growing in popularity. Called the Icelandic Civil Confirmation Program, it consists of an eleven-week educational course on which issues such as ethics, critical thinking, and the meaning of life are discussed.

Graduation

In the past, education in Iceland was a privilege for the few who could afford it. Today it is a right enjoyed by all. Students who graduate from Upper Secondary (the equivalent of High School in the USA) celebrate the completion of their studies by dressing up in costume, usually similarly themed. They have breakfast or lunch together with their teachers, sing songs, and exchange gifts and cards. The school principal addresses the students, congratulates them on their hard-won achievements, and—it is to be hoped—inspires them for the future that awaits them. After this the fun begins, and the students, still in costume, stream into the center of town for an afternoon of celebration and merrymaking, with activities such as bowling, ice skating, and laser tag. Many continue with dinner and further celebrations into the night. The tradition is called Dismission, and some people still nostalgically refer to it as the best day of their lives.

Weddings

The Icelandic word for a wedding is *brúðkaup* which means "buying the bride"—romantic, right? In the past, marriage was a way of connecting families and a means of survival, and as such was not generally entered into by choice. It was not uncommon for a bride and groom to meet for the first time on their wedding day.

Wedding ceremonies would often take place in August, at the end of the slaughter season, when food was plentiful and the weather allowed for travel. The bride would arrive on horseback, with her father at the reins, as would the groom. Traditionally, men and women would celebrate separately, and at the end of the night the groom's guests would jokingly bid for

Iceland is a popular choice for "destination weddings," and it's not difficult to see why.

the bride's virginity. A bridesmaid, whose job it was to choose the "suitor," would pick the groom, who would have prepared a special gift for his bride. A nod to this old-time tradition, called *morgungjöf* (morning gift), still takes place today: the bride and groom exchange gifts the morning after the wedding. The celebrations often continued for a number of days.

Today most weddings take place in a church, though outdoor weddings have also become popular, and the ceremony lasts from thirty minutes to an hour at most. At some weddings, seating inside the church is split by gender, with men sitting on the groom's side, and women on the bride's. The mothers of the couple greet the guests at the entrance, and once all have arrived the father of the bride will escort her up the aisle to the groom and his best man, commonly the groom's father. The brief ritual takes place, some music may be performed before the vows and rings are exchanged, and the ceremony is brought to a close.

Reception parties vary. They can be all-night affairs with music, food, drinking, and dancing, while others may be much shorter, consisting only of the customary speeches, and the serving of coffee and cake—most often a *kransekaka* cake, a tiered sponge cake flavored with marzipan. The cake may be sliced, or people may break off pieces with their hands, but everyone will enjoy it, especially if there's a bottle of wine hidden within!

CHAPTER FOUR

MAKING FRIENDS

Though typically straightforward and easygoing, Icelanders can be difficult to get to know beyond a superficial level. "Stiff" is a word that is sometimes thrown around, and striking up a conversation with a perfect stranger has never been a popular pastime. In much the same way that long, hot summers and blue skies have influenced the extroverted and temperamental demeanor of southern Europeans, it's probably fair to say that Iceland's long, dark, and frigid winters have something to do with the stoic coolness and seeming impenetrability of its inhabitants. It's not all doom and gloom, though; friendship with an Icelander is much like a hike up a frozen volcanic glacier—it may take a while, but it is well worth the effort.

Icelandic friends are down-to-earth, honest, curious, and extremely dependable, and friendships are highly valued, which explains why they are not made overnight. In a natural environment as inhospitable as this, for centuries one's very survival would often depend on having a solid network of friends upon whom you could rely in times of need.

Helpfully, today you don't need to speak Icelandic to connect with people here, as English is widely spoken, though knowing even a few words or phrases would certainly work in your favor (see page 182). When initiating conversations and taking the first steps, perseverance pays.

BREAKING THE ICE

For most Icelanders, social circles are established early in life, and are usually lifelong. Friends will be made at university and at work, but it can be hard to form new friendships outside those environments. If you are going to be spending more than a short time on the island, then by far the best place to meet some of the locals is at clubs and groups where people get together to pursue a common interest or hobby. Whatever the setting, when it comes to breaking the ice and striking up a conversation, there are a few things to keep in mind.

Being descendants of Germanic tribes, most Icelanders don't naturally talk about their feelings or express their emotions. This may change once a friendship has developed, but until that happens people prefer to stick to

People socializing on a sunny day in Reykjavik.

lighter and more general topics of conversation, such as common interests, culture, travel experiences, current affairs, and sports—developing an interest in handball, the national sport, will serve you well!

Icelanders are actually good conversationalists, and very much enjoy an exchange of ideas and opinions with others. Just don't wait for someone else to start the conversation, because you may end up waiting a very long time. During the winter, cozy cafés are popular with locals seeking shelter from the cold and darkness outside, and in Reykjavik there are many to choose from. Become a regular at one or two spots, and you will soon be meeting other locals.

Evening outings to bars, music venues, and clubs are the occasions when you will find the Icelanders at their most outgoing. Yes, it probably has something to do with the quantity of alcohol consumed, but the atmosphere is good-natured, the smiles genuine, and the conversation free flowing. Overall, the Icelanders are very casual about their socializing, so a little initiative will go a long way.

HOSPITALITY

An Invitation Home

Icelandic people enjoy inviting friends over for dinner, and this is preferred to going out for a meal. Most invitations home will take place on a Friday or Saturday, as socializing is generally kept to a minimum mid-week, and Sundays are often spent with family. It is normal to arrive about half an hour *after* the time you were invited for—there are no prizes for being punctual, and certainly none for being early. A gift, such as a bottle of wine, will always be gladly received, but is not expected. The most important (and possibly only) point of etiquette to remember when visiting an Icelandic home takes place before you've even entered the building: always, without fail, take off your shoes. As discussed in the next chapter, the Icelanders are very particular about the cleanliness of their homes, and to walk into someone's home with your shoes on would be disrespectful.

How you greet people once inside depends on how well you know each other. A firm handshake and steady eye contact while saying hello is the norm, and a failsafe for acquaintances, both men and women. Among friends, however, a hug and a kiss on the cheek between women, and a kiss on the cheek between friends of the opposite sex, is common. Take your cue from your hosts, and if in doubt a solid handshake will always go down well. When it comes to food, either your host will serve you or there will be a table from which people are free to take what they like. There will always be plenty to eat, and going in for a second helping is perfectly acceptable.

It's common for guests to stay around for some conversation after the meal, and not be in a rush to leave. When it is time to leave, along with another handshake, hug, kiss, or some combination thereof, the usual word for "Goodbye" is "*Bless,*" to which the response is "*Bless bless,*" and "*Sjáumst!*" which means "See you!"

GOING OUT

The ever-present attitude of *thetta reddast* means that making plans in advance can be tricky. It's always best to confirm things nearer the time, as verbal arrangements are not necessarily considered set in stone. When meeting up with a friend, it's quite normal for people to turn up fifteen to thirty minutes after the arranged time, so don't be offended if you find yourself waiting, or if they don't apologize when they do eventually arrive—it's just the way things are.

The most popular time for socializing is on weekends, when people may go out together for a meal, a drink, or to enjoy some music. Considering its size, Reykjavik has a respectable number of popular bars and clubs, the majority of which are concentrated around the main central shopping street, Laugavegur—the perfect place for a good night out. There is rarely an entrance fee, dress codes are casual (except at a couple of specific venues), and lines, if any, are short. As drinks are pricey, some prefer to gather at a friend's house before heading out. Once out, it is quite common to move from one venue to the next, enjoying the different genres and atmospheres on offer. On the weekend most places only really get going at about midnight and will stay open until 5:00 a.m., for those who can manage it. On weeknights places start to close down at 1:00 a.m.

There are good restaurants, too, around Laugavegur. Fridays and Saturdays have always been the most popular nights for going out, though Thursdays and Sundays have also become "little Saturdays" for those whose schedules can accommodate this.

When it comes to paying the bill, each person will pay for what he or she has had.

DATING

Asked to describe Iceland's dating culture, the author's wife, a non-native Icelander, succinctly summed proceedings up as "sex at night, coffee in the morning." A slight oversimplification of mating habits on the fifty-third latitude perhaps, but it serves to illustrate how attitudes to these matters in Iceland are as characteristically informal as so many other things on the island.

To many Icelanders, the very concept of a "date" feels somewhat ceremonial, and trying to arrange one is not a popular or common way to go about meeting a romantic partner. When you do meet someone you like there is little etiquette to be aware of other than that demanded by basic good manners. Some may find reading the intentions of potential partners tricky when there are no rules of engagement to speak of, and so being upfront in communicating is key, and expected. Attitudes to sex are relaxed, and sexual relations needn't imply any other ambitions. Icelandic men are not known for giving compliments, but after a drink or two they will certainly try, and women in turn are not judged for shopping around or making the first move. As anywhere, phone apps such as Tinder have become popular and are an easy way to meet someone for a date—just don't call it a date!

CLUBS AND SOCIETIES

As we've discussed, the Icelanders are not ones to rush into new friendships. With so many tourists flocking to the country it is perhaps understandable that, for locals, making friends with a visitor has lost some of the appeal it once held; after all, what's the point if the person is only staying in the country for a few days? If you are staying in Iceland for the medium to long

term, then the best way to get around this problem and into local life is to join a hobby or sports group, of which there are very many.

One particularly popular choice is to join a choir, of which there are dozens in Reykjavik alone. Local churches, the universities, schools, women-only choirs, men-only choirs, mixed ones—the choice is vast, and it's highly recommended as a fun way to meet people regularly. You will also be able to practice your Icelandic. In fact, adding an Icelandic language class to your schedule is another way to meet new people—largely other expats who are also looking for new friends—and it will earn you some serious points with the locals, who will understand that your intentions to become involved in the life and culture of the country are serious.

There are many other interest clubs or groups—for board games, sewing, swimming, football, handball, horse riding, and more—where people mix and socialize. Facebook can be a very helpful resource for seeing what's available and making initial contact.

CHAPTER FIVE

THE ICELANDERS AT HOME

In general, the Icelandic people enjoy a very high quality of life. Despite above-average living costs and long working hours for many, Iceland routinely measures highly against OECD quality-of-life criteria, and it's not hard to see why. The environment is clean, and the exceptional beauty of the natural landscape provides plenty of opportunities for outdoor recreation and exercise. Natural spring water gushes out of the faucets, while the majority of homes enjoy low-cost and renewably sourced heating, courtesy of the country's geothermal water stores. A robust welfare and social support system provides a safety net upon which people can rely, should they need to. Having an exceptionally low level of crime, Iceland is also a very safe place to live, and Icelandic children are afforded a greater level of freedom and responsibility than their peers elsewhere in Western Europe.

Houses in the western town of Stykkishólmur.

HOUSING

Knowing what we do about the Icelanders' need for independence and the value they place on being self-reliant, it is no surprise, perhaps, that the majority want to own their homes. Today, there is an 80 percent ownership rate—among the highest in the world. The crash of 2008 saw a number of homes repossessed when the devaluation of the krona meant that keeping up mortgage repayments became impossible for some. The post-crash recovery was quick, however, and it didn't take long for normal business to resume, including within the housing market. Today the lack of suitable and affordable rental options has become

the subject of debate as rising house prices have made affordability an issue for low-income earners and those below the age of thirty. While there is support for increasing government-subsidized social housing, most people will still try to get on the property ladder as soon as they can afford to.

The material standards of homes in Iceland are high. The environment means good insulation and season-appropriate lighting are key, including being able to block out daylight during nighttime hours in the summer. While cement for construction was produced locally until the early nineteenth century, today it is imported, along with the majority of other building materials, as the cost of local production is prohibitive. Apartments are the norm in downtown Reykjavik, where space comes at a premium, while in rural areas the majority of houses are large, making use of the abundance of space available. Steaming geothermal water heats 90 percent of Icelandic homes; you'll get used to the sulfur-like smell when you shower—hydrogen sulfide is added to the water to make sure that all oxygen is removed to prevent pipes and radiators from corroding. It's completely harmless, so don't worry if you swallow a mouthful. Ninety-five percent of the cold water in Iceland's faucets comes from natural springs. Clean and healthy, it is free of chlorine, fluoride, and calcium—just let it run for a moment to clear the hot water out of the pipes and get rid of the smell.

There isn't a great deal of variation when it comes to exterior and interior design. Blue, red, or brown outer walls paired with simple white interior walls are the norm, though more variety can be found in Reykjavik, particularly downtown, where some cafés and shops have preserved older styles that were built before the introduction of planning laws.

Cleanliness is important to Icelanders, and most of the homes you visit will be well kept and uncluttered. Don't forget to remove your shoes when entering anyone's home! Cleaning one's own home is usual. In a society that sees itself as deeply egalitarian (see Chapter 2), there is some stigma attached to

Many families in Iceland own second homes. Most often in rural locations, they are where people like to go to spend the holidays if they can.

employing a person to clean up after you. This attitude has softened in recent years, however, and using hired help has become more common, even if people aren't as comfortable talking about it as openly as they are elsewhere.

Owning a second home is common in Iceland, and families will retreat to a holiday home in the period around Christmas and in the summer, often inviting their extended family and friends to join them. A steaming outdoor Jacuzzi in the snow is something you can look forward to if you are lucky enough to swing an invite!

THE FAMILY UNIT

Icelandic families come in many shapes and sizes. As previously discussed, marriage, as a means of legally formalizing a couple's union, is not seen as integral to a long and meaningful relationship, and certainly not as a prerequisite to having children. A majority of couples in Iceland are happy to cohabit and have children long before considering whether or not to tie the knot. For couples that do eventually get married, it is often out of practical considerations relating to inheritance, as those in "consensual unions," (couples registered as living together but not legally married) do not have the same legal protection when it comes to a breakdown of the relationship, or the death of a partner, as those who are married.

Iceland's history offers some clues to the prevalence of these popular yet seemingly unconventional family arrangements. In the distant past, marriage was a privilege granted only to those who owned land, as a way of preventing overpopulation in a resource-scarce society. Though no such legal requirement has existed for more than two hundred years, the social patterns persist, and the modern institution of marriage has never acquired the same importance as it has in other countries.

One result of this is that the majority of Icelandic children are born out of wedlock, and blended families living under one roof are very much the norm. In general, grandparents and other relatives are used to accepting new members into the family, and in most cases children from a previous relationship will become fully accepted members of the new stepparent's family. Families with same-sex parents have also become more common.

Fertility rates have been in free fall since the 1960s, and are now at an all-time low of 1.7 children per woman—a pattern that is mirrored in much of Europe and Scandinavia. This has not yet affected

Iceland's population level, largely due to the increase in life expectancy; however, that may change if the birth rate continues to decline. Such a trend will mean difficulties for the economy in future, as there will be a reduced working population to support those who are no longer working.

GROWING UP IN ICELAND

Iceland is an exceptionally safe country, and has one of the lowest crime rates in the world. As a result, children benefit from a great amount of freedom to play and roam, and are given opportunities to look after themselves and develop a sense of self-reliance to an extent that has become rare in many Western countries, particularly in large cities. Icelandic children as young as six will walk by themselves to school and back, and young children are left to play and explore outdoors.

Take a walk down a busy street in Reykjavik, and you may be surprised to see babies left alone to nap in their strollers. Even more surprising, perhaps, is that this is also true during wintertime—leaving babies outside to sleep in all seasons has been practiced for many centuries in Iceland. The parents may be close by but are content to carry on with whatever else they are doing and leave their babies in outdoor public

The neighborhood gang surveys its territory.

spaces. This says much about Iceland's social fabric and the level of mutual trust among its citizens.

Teenagers, too, are given more freedom than their peers in other countries, and there is great appreciation and encouragement for their independence. It is common for those as young as fourteen to start earning money through menial work, and summer jobs are popular—as cashiers in supermarkets, as cleaners for a local municipality, or as farm hands. In 2018 one in four under-eighteens were on the payroll, including some seven hundred children as young as twelve. In a society where people value independence and self-reliance above all else, this probably shouldn't be surprising, and adults who themselves will have started work as teenagers will happily tout the benefits of becoming responsible and learning to manage money at a young age. Luckily, in most cases, it doesn't come at the expense of a healthy amount of time for rest and play.

DAILY LIFE

For most, the working day typically starts at 7:00 or 7:30 a.m. Breakfast is usually eaten at home, and may consist of *hafragrautur*, a traditional porridge usually topped with brown sugar, raisins, or butter, *skyr,* a deliciously thick, yoghurt-like cheese made from strained skimmed milk, or just a bowl of cereal. Children are dispatched to school, and most people arrive at work between 8:00 and 9:00 a.m. Lunch breaks at work are usually thirty minutes to an hour long, and if you work for a large company there is often a canteen that caters to all the staff. For those who work for smaller companies, a quick lunch at a local eatery, a sandwich, or a packed lunch from home is the norm. Those who live close enough to their work may also head home for lunch. Per capita, the Icelanders are the fourth-largest consumers of coffee on the planet, and the working day provides multiple opportunities to ensure that this remains the case. Work usually finishes between 4:00 and 5:00 p.m., but, particularly for those in the private sector, working overtime is common and does not represent a problem as in some other Scandinavian countries, where the need to work overtime expresses an inability to get your work done in the allotted time.

With such long working hours, weekday evenings are reserved for rest and relaxation at home, particularly during the winter months. Going out for a drink after work with colleagues or friends isn't unheard of, but it is not nearly as common as it is in many other countries. On the whole, socializing, either at home or outside, is kept for the weekends.

CULINARY QUIRKS

Icelandic cuisine doesn't have a great reputation. As we have seen, traditional dishes include pickled ram's testicles, fermented shark, and boiled lamb's head cured in lactic acid. It's probably best not to try them all at the same sitting.

In its defense, it's worth bearing in mind that, for most of its history, Iceland was extremely isolated— its nearest neighbors are hundreds of miles away.

From top to bottom: Dried stockfish, best enjoyed smothered with butter; local langoustine lobster served with salad and cream; *kjötsúpa*, braised lamb soup with root vegetables.

Fresh food was hard to come by, so nutrition was taken wherever it was found. Thankfully, things have come a long way since then, and contemporary Icelandic cuisine has a lot going for it. Indeed, it is experiencing something of a renaissance; an abundance of fresh seafood, free-range lamb, and wild berries are just some of the highlights.

Iceland has never been self-sufficient in grain, and until the nineteenth century bread was very much a luxury. Dried stockfish (*harðfiskur*) was the traditional staple; filleted, salty, and often smothered in butter, it was often eaten as an accompaniment to the main dish, usually fish or lamb. Today, however, bread is no longer a rarity and is widely eaten. Some breads unique to the island include *laufabrauð*, leafbread, traditionally eaten at Christmas time (see page 78), and *hverabrauð*, a dark, sweet-tasting rye bread traditionally prepared by burying the baking pot near a hot spring and letting the geothermal heat do the cooking.

Sweet treats, such as *pönnukökur*, thin, crêpe-like pancakes eaten with whipped cream and jam, are widely enjoyed, and ice cream is something of a national obsession, even in winter. Those with a sweet tooth will enjoy *nammi* with *ís*—ice cream topped with candy and copious quantities of sauce!

EVERYDAY SHOPPING

Things are expensive in Iceland, including everyday necessities such as groceries, clothing, and transportation. For locals at least, there has been some improvement in recent years. Spending power has increased, and people now spend a smaller proportion of their income on basic goods than they have had to in the past. Whatever your budget, though, there are ways to be smart about shopping, and large supermarket chains, such as Bonus, are the cheapest places for all your daily and weekly shopping needs. The advent of

these giant supermarkets, however, has seen mom-and-pop grocery stores all but disappear from Iceland's high streets. Having your groceries delivered to your home is an option, though not necessarily a popular one, except with senior citizens, for whom it is a great help. During the week, most high street shops open between 9:00 and 10:00 a.m., usually until 6:00 p.m. On the weekend things get going a little later; most shops will open between 10:00 and 11:00 a.m. and close between 2:00 and 5:00 p.m., depending on the shop. (For more on shopping, see Chapter Six.)

EDUCATION

As in other Nordic countries, there is free and mandatory education in Iceland for all children aged between six and sixteen. Before starting school many children will attend a pre-school, most of which are heavily subsidized by the state. Education beyond sixteen, known as "upper secondary," is also state funded, and is open to all those who complete their compulsory education. Students at upper-secondary level have the option of pursuing vocational training. With such a comprehensive and successful state education system, privately funded schools are a rarity.

All upper-secondary graduates are entitled to study at any of the country's four public universities,

The University of Iceland, Reykjavik: Iceland's oldest institution of higher learning.

which, except for a registration fee, are entirely free. The academic year runs from September to May, and is split into a fall term and a spring term. Exchange students from abroad account for approximately 5 percent of Iceland's university students.

Approximately 30 percent of Icelandic men aged between twenty-four and sixty are university graduates. For women the figure is substantially higher, at more than 50 percent.

THE UNIVERSITY OF ICELAND

There are seven universities in Iceland, four of which are public and three of which are private. Among them, the University of Iceland remains the principal institution for higher learning in the country. Founded on June 17, 1911, the centenary of the birth of independence hero Jon Sigurdsson, its first cohort of students consisted of forty-four men and one woman. Today women make up 66 percent of university graduates in Iceland. With nearly 3,000 teachers and hundreds of researchers and administrators, the University of Iceland is the country's largest single workplace. The university enjoys a thriving student community, with more than sixty unions in operation on campus. Its largest campus, situated in the center of Reykjavik, consists of some thirty buildings spread over about twenty-five acres (10 hectares). Popular faculties include Social Sciences, Health Sciences, Education, Engineering, and Natural Sciences.

CHAPTER SIX

TIME OUT

As we have seen, Icelanders enjoy standards well above the European average in a number of key fields: the environment, employment, community, affluence, and health. One area, however, in which they do not perform well is their work–life balance. It is very common for Icelanders to work longer hours than workers in any other country in Europe, at the expense of leisure time. A forty-five-hour working week is common, and one person in seven works more than fifty hours a week. Putting in additional hours and working overtime is par for the course. According to the OECD, Icelanders devote ninety minutes less per day to leisure and personal matters than their Scandinavian counterparts in Denmark. Public awareness of the negative effects of working long hours is increasing, and people are looking at practical ways to achieve a better balance. Many would argue that a technologically developed country

Bathers enjoy the warm, mineral-rich waters at the Blue Lagoon geothermal spa in Grindavik, southwest Iceland.

as full of natural resources as Iceland should be able to afford its people more time off.

With free time in short supply, the Icelanders have learned how to make the most of it, and there is a wealth of activities on offer, both indoors and out. If you are visiting Iceland for a short while, you can purchase a City Card at Reykjavik's City Hall, which will give you free or discounted access to, or use of, many of the country's best museums, restaurants, city tours, swimming pools, and buses.

PUBLIC BATHING

Iceland is not just the land of fire and ice—truly, it's a land of fire, ice, and wonderfully warm geothermal

springs. Whether in outdoor pools and man-made beaches, or in bubbling lagoons and geothermal rivers, Icelanders have enjoyed swimming and bathing for centuries, and this is how many like to unwind, whatever the time of year. What could be more relaxing than taking a dip in a steaming outdoor tub in the middle of winter and looking up at the night sky sparkling with stars, while snowflakes gently drop onto your nose?

The Icelanders take their bathing seriously, and high levels of hygiene are maintained at all public pools. The use of chlorine is kept to an absolute minimum—in many cases, none is used at all—so bathers are required to wash in showers provided before entering the water. Men and women shower separately, and most will shower naked. If you are shy, don't worry; taking public showers naked is the norm and an entirely mundane act in Iceland—everyone simply minds their own business. Once washed and in your bathing suit, you are permitted to enter the water. Women are not required to cover their breasts at public springs, and, though most do, bathing topless will not attract attention.

Except for in the wildest spots, most bathing pools, man-made or natural, will have facilities such as saunas, steam baths, cafés, and clean changing rooms where you can leave your belongings. Bathers pay an entrance fee that goes toward the upkeep of the facilities. For those with enough time and a sense of adventure there are numerous wild springs dotted around the country. There won't be any facilities there, but there are unlikely to be any other people either.

DINING OUT

When this author was growing up in Iceland in the '80s dining out was a rare experience. One might have eaten at a restaurant once a month if money allowed, but in any case dining options were limited: burgers with chips and a small selection of lamb or beef dishes were the extent of the variety. Pizza did not arrive on the scene until the late 1980s, and cuisine from other parts of the world was still sorely lacking. The restaurant scene

Diners make the most of the good weather at the Hannes Boy Cafe in Siglufjörður, northern Iceland.

only really began to improve in the '90s, when an increasing number of immigrants brought with them new flavors and dishes that were appreciated by locals and visitors alike. Middle Eastern, Southeast Asian, and African restaurants all became part of the culinary landscape. Today there is an abundance of restaurants to choose from that cater to every taste, as well as a growing number of vegetarian and vegan eateries. The selection outside Reykjavik is more limited, but you'll be pleasantly surprised at what you can find in the larger villages.

Cafés have become popular too, and there is a vibrant café scene in Reykjavik, particularly in the

city center (with not a single Starbucks to be found!).
Most cafés also serve food, and if you're in the mood
for something sweet, try some Icelandic chocolate—
import restrictions in the past meant Iceland
developed many of its own local brands—or a local
pastry like *kleina*, a deep-fried, doughy delight.

While there are restaurants for different budgets,
dining out is expensive, as with most things in Iceland.
The country has always had to rely on importing most
of its food, and high tariffs put in place to protect local
agriculture further add to the cost of transportation
for a great deal of produce. This is one reason you will
see so many visitors stocking up at Bonus, Iceland's
only budget supermarket chain. When you are in
Reykjavik, the Craving app will help you locate the
nearest restaurants and provide you with information
such as what's on offer, the cost, and reviews.

It is probably worth mentioning that internationally
popular fast-food chains like McDonald's or Burger
King do not operate in Iceland. Rather, it is the
humble hot dog which is the fast-food of choice here.
These are widely available and much beloved by locals,
who are happy to enjoy them at any time of day, while
travelers appreciate their price. In addition to the usual
condiments like ketchup, mayonnaise, and mustard,
hot dogs in Iceland are popularly eaten with both raw
and crispy fried onions, as well as a sweet mayonnaise-
based relish called *remúlaði* (known as remoulade

Quick, hot, and saucy; hotdogs have a special place in the heart of many Icelanders.

elsewhere) that is made with capers, sweet mustard, and herbs. If you like the sound of all that, you can ask the server for "*ein með öllu*," which means "one with everything."

ALCOHOL

The Icelanders like to drink. In the past, the local drinking culture was not a healthy one: binge drinking on the weekends was common, and closing time at 3:00 a.m. often meant the start of fights and general drunken rowdiness. In fact, drinking oneself to oblivion became an activity so widespread that in 1915 the government introduced a total prohibition on alcohol.

Distilled from wheat and barley, locally produced Reyka vodka is made with glacial water and filtered through lava rock.

Spirits were legalized again in 1933, but beer remained illegal until as late as 1989. Things have improved markedly in recent decades, and the majority of younger Icelanders don't drink to excess.

The price of alcohol means that those going out for an evening often start off with a pre-drink or two with friends at someone's house. Things only really start to get going at about 11:00 p.m., which is when most people head out.

THEATER AND CINEMA

Iceland's oldest theater, the Reykjavik City Theater, dates back to 1897. What started as a small, poky, wooden structure is today a multistage performance complex that can host audiences of 1,000. Here you can find international and local productions, both mainstream and left-field. An integral part of Icelandic cultural life, the theater also hosts public talks and musical concerts. Iceland's National Theater stages a varied offering of Icelandic and foreign productions, classics, musicals, operas, and children's productions. Located in Reykjavik's historical center, the theater was designed by state architect Gudjon Samuelsson as a "Palace of Elves." An unassuming and unembellished basalt structure, the design references the ancient Icelandic belief that elves live inside rocks and suggests that the humans inside the theater could enter the elvish world through drama, dance, and song. A visit to the theater is popular across all levels of society, and, though people will often dress in smart-casual attire when attending a performance, there is no formal dress code. In all there are about twenty professional theaters around the country, and dozens of drama societies. While most performances are in Icelandic, there are also English productions.

With its striking landscape, Iceland has become a popular location for international production companies looking for dramatic and otherworldly backdrops for their films. At the same time, with strong support from the state, a local Icelandic film industry has firmly found its feet, and the country has a steady stream of homegrown feature-length and

The National Theater, Reykjavik.

short releases every year. Household names include
Fridrik Thor Fridriksson, whose 1991 production
Children of Nature, about an elderly couple who retreat
into the wilderness to die together, won an Oscar
Academy award for best foreign-language film; and
Isold Uggadottir, who picked up the Directing Award
for World Cinema for her film *And Breathe Normally*
at the Sundance Festival in 2018. Film lovers should
head to Iceland's independent arthouse cinema, the
Bio Paradis, in downtown Reykjavik, which offers
Icelandic and foreign productions and a cozy bar.

One of the calendar highlights for Icelandic cinema is the Reykjavik International Film Festival, which, spread over eleven days in the fall, offers film viewings in some unique settings, including swimming pools, caves, and the homes of local filmmakers.

ART

Iceland's art scene is colorful and varied, and a point of pride for many locals. Reykjavik is home to a number of high-quality galleries and exhibition spaces, many of which are well worth a visit. A good place to start is the Reykjavik Art Museum, which showcases

The iconic Sun Voyager in Reykjavik, by sculptor Jon Gunnar Arnason.

works by some of Iceland's best-known modern and contemporary artists, including Erro, Kjarval, and Asmundur Sveinsson, as well as works by international and up-and-coming local artists. Spread over three sites, there is much to see, including sculptures, paintings, and more experimental installations. One ticket grants admission to all three sites over the course of a day, but bear in mind that they are not within easy walking distance of one another. The restaurant at the Harbor House (Hafnarhús) building, with views over Reykjavik's old harbor, is a pleasant spot for lunch. The museum also hosts a number of cultural events, including musical performances and seminars throughout the year. Other notable galleries include the nearby i8 Gallery, which shows international and local contemporary art, and Gallerí Fold, Iceland's principal auction house. There are four galleries spread over nearly 6,500 square feet (about 600 sq. meters) of exhibition space, and admission is free.

Outside Reykjavik are a number of interesting art venues that are notable for the quality and variety of their offerings. In the northernmost city of Akureyri, the recently refurbished Akureyri Art Museum showcases both local and national talent and runs a guided tour in English every Thursday. On the east coast, in the tiny town of Seydisfordur, is the Skaftfell Center for Visual Arts, which offers an eclectic and impressive collection, particularly considering the remoteness of its location. The institution also offers an artist's residency program, giving artists from all over the world the opportunity to stay in the village for an extended period in order to experiment and develop their craft.

LITERATURE

Iceland is proud of its literary heritage, of which the thirteenth-century Sagas are the earliest and best-known examples. The Sagas are familiar to all Icelanders, and their influence on culture and identity have been far reaching; indeed, the heroes and antiheroes of those epic tales contributed to an Icelandic self-image that was mobilized in the struggle for political independence.

One modern Icelandic literary treasure is Halldór Laxness, who was awarded the Nobel Prize for Literature in 1955. Though in his early years the laureate apparently didn't think much of the Sagas—or "those old Icelandic fogeys," as he described them in a letter to a friend in 1913—the Swedish Academy credited him with having successfully renewed Iceland's great narrative art. Dubbed "the Tolstoy of the North," Laxness wrote highly acclaimed works such as *Salka Valka*, *Independent People*, and

World Light—darkly humorous and somewhat tragic studies of Iceland's social tensions, and the poverty and aspirations of its rural inhabitants.

Iceland's contemporary literary scene is thriving. The country publishes around 1,300 books every year—a remarkable figure for a population of only 350,000, and the highest figure per capita for any country in the world. A book is very much a valued gift in Iceland, and many will spend Christmas Eve with a book gifted to them by a friend or relative.

MUSIC AND FESTIVALS

In Iceland it is said that even the most boring people become fun when they join a choir, and there must be some truth in it—nearly every town in Iceland has at least one active choir and there are more than three hundred countrywide, so they must be doing something right. Joining a choir is a great way to meet people if you are new in town, and people take part in them for the social benefits as much as for the musical enjoyment. Most choirs work toward a number of public performances each year, such as at Christmas and in the spring, and many will travel abroad together to perform.

Iceland's musical traditions stretch back a long way—one can hear folk songs circulating today that originated in the fourteenth century. There are traditional forms of singing, such as *kveða* (rhythmic chanting) and *tvísöngur* (singing in parallel fifths) as well as local traditional instruments such as the *langspil* (a type of drone zither) and a *fiðla* (the Icelandic fiddle). Iceland's contemporary music scene is amazingly diverse, particularly given its size, and has produced a few well-known artists on the world stage, including Bjork and Sigur Ros. More recently, the Reykjavik-based band Of Monsters and Men, famous for their brand of Indie pop and folk music, achieved over a billion Spotify plays, the first and only Icelandic band to do so. Perhaps Iceland's music scene is actually helped by its limited size; due to short supply musicians are well practiced in playing across genres, and the scene has lent itself to the creation of boundary-breaking popular music not found elsewhere.

Many music festivals take place throughout the year, and in Reykjavik live music can be found on most nights of the week. A good place to start is Harpa, a concert hall whose schedule can be viewed online. Other live music venues in Reykjavik include bars such as Húrra, Kex, and Iðnó, all of which offer live music from a range of genres in informal settings. Tjarnarbíó hosts both music and theatrical performances, while Gaukurinn is the place to visit if heavy metal is your thing—it is also a drag-scene favorite!

A number of music festivals are well worth checking out. The most popular ones include the

Top to bottom: The Harpa Concert Hall, Reykjavik, and its interior; local musicians perform on the the street in Reykjavik.

Sónar Reykjavík festival in February, the Secret Solstice festival in June, and the Iceland Airways festival in November. There are many smaller festivals held throughout the year and across the country, including "Aldrei fór ég suður" ("I've never headed South"), a free three-day rock festival in the Westfjords region at Easter.

The month of August, especially the bank holiday weekend, is extremely popular for camping festivals around the country, and they are highly recommended if you are in Iceland during this time. There are a number of good online resources to check for listings, including www.guidetoiceland.is.

SPORTS AND EXERCISE

The Icelanders are an active bunch, and have a great love of the outdoors and physical exercise in general. Iceland's ancient Sagas tell of tall and powerful heroes, and the unforgiving environment meant that in the past physical prowess was necessary for survival. Reykjavik's washerwomen were known to walk for miles to the nearest suitable water while carrying their laundry and equipment, while fishermen were deemed worthy if they could lift the heaviest stones. That said, not everyone you meet will be a strongman (though all will know and love the original strongman, Jon Pall Sigmarsson): Icelanders still drink more Coke per capita than anyone else in the world, and until 1983 the country's sole television station ceased programming in the month of July in an effort to get people off the couch. Television was banned on Thursdays until 1987 for the same reason. Today, there is widespread appreciation of what constitutes a healthy lifestyle and poor weather conditions are not usually a hindrance—it's just a question of wearing the right clothing.

Hiking and walking are popular forms of exercise, as are horse riding, rock climbing, swimming, soccer, and handball, which is the national sport. Gyms are widely used, particularly during the winter, when people like

Handball, Iceland's national sport.

to take part in yoga sessions (especially hot yoga) and spinning in addition to regular weight training. Glima, a unique form of wrestling brought over by the Vikings, is still practiced today by both men and women. (For more on what Iceland's great outdoors has to offer, see Chapter 7.)

ANGLING

With hundreds of rivers and lakes and a wide variety of fish, angling has become a very popular outdoor activity in Iceland. It is, however, subject to much regulation, and is not a cheap pastime. The rivers in Iceland are privately owned, and landowners, often farmers, usually lease the land to angling organizations who issue licenses to their members. Licenses are expensive, and each site will have rules about when you can fish, what bait is allowed, and whether or not you are permitted to take your catch home. Sea trout, river trout, salmon, and the prized arctic char are all popular catches, though they come with vastly differing price tags. For those who are interested, the Reykjavik Angling Club can assist with information and licenses.

SHOPPING FOR PLEASURE

Icelandic design has developed on the solid foundations of Nordic style—minimalism, simplicity, and functionality—but has a twist all of its own. Forward, off-beat, and inspired by the country's unique natural environment, it is a pleasure to explore. One of the best places to do so is in Laugavegur, Reykjavik's main shopping thoroughfare. Here you will find shops selling the best that Icelandic designers have to offer, from fashion to homeware, alongside restaurants, cafés, and bars.

The nearby Kringlan mall has more than 180 shops that feature both national and international brands, as well as restaurants and a cinema. Smaralind, Iceland's largest mall, is located about four and a half miles (7 km) from Reykjavik's city center.

For more traditional Icelandic items, including crafts, delicacies (fermented shark, anyone?), homeware, clothing, and souvenirs, Reykjavik's flea market, Kolaportið, located at the old harbor, is an excellent place to start. It is also the one place in Iceland where you can haggle, particularly if it's a Sunday evening when the vendors are already thinking of home.

Frú Lauga Farmers' Market store in the city center is another destination worth visiting. It sells local foods including dairy products and meat sourced from Iceland's best farms. Not too far from here you will find the Hlemmur Food Hall. Housing ten different vendors, it is a good spot to sample some of the best food around.

MONEY MATTERS

Iceland is not a cashless society quite yet, but it does seem to be heading that way. Card payments are the norm, and most people don't expect to need cash when they are out and about. There has been some resistance to going entirely electronic, though—there was a public outcry when one center-right politician recently suggested the country should do so in order to help prevent tax fraud. The topic is a good illustration of some of the forces at play in Iceland today: yes, modernity and technological advancement are embraced, but it is tempered by conservative attitudes, and most older Icelanders feel more comfortable having at least the option of being able to use "old-fashioned" paper money. For those who have grown up with the Internet, and for whom a cell phone is more akin to a fifth limb than a communication device, swiping and clicking are entirely natural means of commerce and, as elsewhere in the world, this may eventually spell the demise of hard currency in Iceland in the future. Make sure that your credit or debit card is PIN-ready before you land in Iceland to allow for payment by card to be made.

CHAPTER SEVEN

TRAVEL, HEALTH, & SAFETY

There is much to see in Iceland, and it is usual for visitors to spend far more time outside Reykjavik than in it, discovering the fjords, glaciers, springs, volcanoes, and black sand beaches that make the island unique. Though weather conditions can sometimes disrupt travel plans, particularly in the highlands, the roads are generally well maintained and allow for countrywide exploration with relative ease.

DRIVING

Iceland has an extensive road network, and most of the country is accessible by car or public bus. The core of the road network is made up of Primary Roads, including the Ring Road, Iceland's main artery, which circles the entire island. Primary Roads connect the majority of Iceland's towns and municipalities, as well as any villages with more than a hundred inhabitants. Most of these roads are paved, but not all. Some Primary Roads run through the highlands, but service is limited on these roads, and they are closed during the winter. Primary Highland Roads are usually narrow gravel roads or tracks, and there are no bridges over most of the rivers there, so one has to drive through them! Secondary Roads connect places inhabited by fewer than a hundred people, travel hubs, and popular tourist destinations to Primary Roads. Some mountains and moors have roads categorized only as Highway Roads, which usually consist of rough, narrow passes and should not be taken by inexperienced drivers or those who do not know

"F" roads; not for the faint hearted.

where they are going. These roads are marked with the letter "F."

Icelandic weather is renowned for its unpredictability. Blizzards and snowstorms can happen suddenly, and wet and icy conditions make for hazardous driving. The speed limit is 90 kmph (60 mph), and it is advisable to respect that, though you may see many native drivers exceeding the limit. Most roads are single-lane only.

Make sure that your credit card is PIN-ready, as many gas stations cannot accept card payment otherwise. If your card is not PIN-ready, you can purchase prepaid cards for gas for use at isolated gas stations in case you are short of cash. These can be bought at supermarkets and gas stations, and money loaded on to the card for later use.

Check www.road.is for information on routes and live updates on driving conditions around the country.

Renting a Car

Levels of car ownership in Iceland are very high. According to recent figures, there are currently more registered cars than people. For those who would like to explore the country's otherworldly landscapes at their own pace, rental options are abundant, but choosing the right car is important. A two-wheel drive is fine if you plan to stick to the Ring Road, but if you dream of anything more adventurous, then a four-wheel drive is a must. It won't be cheap, and neither will the "gravel protection" insurance excess that you will be recommended to take—but people don't come to Iceland for "cheap," do they?

It's usual to pick up your rental car on arrival at Keflavik International Airport (KEF), approximately forty-five minutes from Reykjavik, which saves you having to take a bus into the capital or arrange a transfer. Drivers must be over the age of twenty-one, or over twenty-five to drive a four-wheel drive, and if your license is not in English (or another language that uses the Latin alphabet), then an international license will be necessary.

Photograph any marks on the car at the time of rental for your own records.

On the road, make sure you keep an eye on the gas level, and fill up whenever you can. It is a good idea to keep plenty of water, snacks, and extra layers of clothing in the car with you; Iceland's isolated roads mean emergency services may take some time to reach you if you get stuck.

Dial 112 to be connected to emergency services if you need assistance.

TAXIS

A number of private taxi companies operate in Iceland, all of them reliable and all of them expensive.

Among the most popular operators are Hreyfill (+354 5885522) and BSR (+354 5610000). Hreyfill cabs can also be booked via their own app. All taxis are metered and begin at around US $5.50. Airport runs are very expensive, costing anywhere between US $120 to $300. Hail-a-ride apps such as Uber and Lyft do not currently operate in Iceland.

BUSES

For those not driving, buses provide an efficient and economical means of reaching Reykjavik after arrival at Keflavik Airport. Transfer services run by Gray Line, Flybus, and others are usually able to drop passengers directly at their accommodation. Tickets for transfer services can be purchased on arrival but are best booked in advance. The journey takes around forty-five minutes on these buses.

The cheapest way to get to Reykjavik from the airport is a Stræto bus (Iceland's main bus operator), number 55, which runs between the city center and the airport. It is also the longest: the journey takes approximately ninety minutes, end to end. There are only nine buses a day, running from around 6:30 a.m. to 7:30 p.m.

Upon arrival in Reykjavik, Stræto's bright yellow buses are the go-to option for getting around the city, providing a cheap and efficient alternative to taxis—fares for which can quickly mount up. Tickets for these buses can be bought on board, though you must have the exact fare (or be willing to overpay), as the driver is unable to give change. Alternatively, tickets can be purchased on their app, which is available in English. The Strætó app also includes a route planner, travel updates, and a live map so that you can check where your bus is. It's a worthwhile download for those planning to get around with public transportation. Tickets can be purchased in bulk, stored on your phone, and activated for use when needed. All tickets are valid for seventy-five minutes from activation. Wi-fi and electrical sockets are available on long-distance routes.

A handful of other companies also operate long-distance routes around the country. Routes and timetables can be found at www.publiciceland.is. Booking in advance is advised.

AIR

Iceland has no fewer than thirteen domestic airports, and air travel provides locals with an important means of transportation when weather conditions make road travel impossible. Be aware, however, that flight schedules are liable to last-minute changes during the winter period. Keflavik Airport does not serve domestic flights; the closest domestic airport is Reykjavik City Airport, which is located 1.2 miles (2 km) from the city center. Shuttle services transfer passengers between the two hubs. Routes and schedules for all domestic flights can be viewed at www.isavia.is.

To the disappointment of locals and visitors alike, there is no train service in Iceland, and it is unlikely that there ever will be one. There are simply too many cars on the road, and not enough people for it to become a viable option.

PLACES TO VISIT

For lovers of nature and seekers of adventure, Iceland does not disappoint. The busiest travel period is the summer months of June to August. Truthfully, though, the spring months of April to June offer just as many opportunities, but with the added advantage of there being far fewer tourists. For those chasing the Northern Lights, the icy winter months are your very best chance.

Iceland's popular tourist trails are by now well trodden, and for good reason. That said, there are many treasures to be discovered for those willing to venture a little farther afield.

Strokkur geyser erupts.

The South

The city of Reykjavik is the gateway to the south, where glaciers, hot springs, black sand beaches, and a national park await, all within approximately a two-hour drive of the city. Most visitors embark on a trail that includes a stop at all three of these sites, known as the Golden Circle. The closest stop on this three-part trail is Thingvellir (Þingvellir) National Park, birthplace of Iceland's democracy and the world's first parliament, the Althing, in 930 CE. Designated a UNESCO World Heritage Site, the park lies in a rift valley known as the Mid Atlantic Ridge, which marks the boundary between the North American and Eurasian tectonic plates—it is

Gullfoss Waterfall.

the only place on Earth where the ridge can be viewed
above land. These tectonic plates continue to move
apart today at the rate of about three-quarters of an
inch (2 cm) per year, causing the area's volcanic activity.
Thingvellir National Park is also home to Iceland's
largest lake, Thingvallavatn (Þingvallavatn), a popular
scuba-diving spot where you can explore fissures at
the tectonic rifts of Silfra and Davíðsgjá. The Silfra Rift
is considered Iceland's best diving site—the water is
crystal clear and the underwater view spectacular. A
number of companies run diving excursions for those
interested, though diving qualifications are required
(a dry-suit diving certification, or ten logged dry-suit

Diving in the clear waters of the Silfra Rift.

dives within the last two years, confirmed with written proof from a diving instructor).

The fifty-minute drive from Thingvellir to the next stop on the Golden Circle, the Geysir Geothermal Area, is an experience in its own right. The landscape of the Haukadalur Valley, in which it is located, is studded with steaming fumaroles and bubbling pits of mud—the whole area is alive with volcanic activity. Geysers are tube-like holes on the Earth's surface that run deep down into the crust. Water that fills the hole will be heated by molten magma. As the temperature rises, water is shot up into the air until the it is able to drop back below 212°F (100°C). The two main geysers that people come to see here are Geysir, after which the area and indeed all geysers are named (the word comes from Old Norse, meaning to gush or flow), and Strokkur. Strokkur, the smaller of the two, erupts approximately every five to ten minutes, shooting a column of water 100 feet (30 meters) into the air. Geysir has lain largely dormant in recent decades, though when it does go off it puts on a remarkable display; in 2000 it blew up a column of water 400 feet (122 meters) tall. While at the site, look out for the striking azure waters of the hot springs at Konungshver and Blesi—the deep blue is a result of the water's particularly high silica content.

The last stop for most on the Golden Circle is the Gullfoss Waterfall, a ten-minute drive from Geysir. From the dramatic valley in which it is located, you can see all the way to the ice wall of the Langjökull Glacier in the distance. It is the run-off from this glacier that fills the river here, the Hvita, as well as the springs at Geysir and the lake at Thingvellir, via underground channels. During the summer clouds of spray ascend from the double waterfall and catch the sunlight to create delightful, rainbow-colored mists. In the winter the winds are sharp, but you can see large chunks of glacial ice being carried along by the current before crashing into the frigid abyss.

Other noteworthy sites and activities in the south include a visit to the Westmann Islands, a swim in the warm geothermal waters of the Secret Lagoon in Fludir (Iceland's oldest swimming pool), and snowmobiling on the mammoth Langjökull Glacier.

VOLCANOES

A description of southern Iceland would not be complete without a discussion of its volcanoes, most notable among them being Katla, Eyjafjallajökull, and Hekla. Buried beneath the Mýrdalsjökull Glacier, Katla is one of Iceland's most active volcanoes. It has erupted roughly once every forty to eighty years for the past millennium and, having last erupted in 1918, is now well overdue for its next eruption. Seismic activity suggests that a further eruption is indeed looking increasingly likely, but the concern this causes in Iceland is fairly subdued. Detailed evacuation plans are in place for all the local communities, as is training, and drills are carried out regularly. It is also worth mentioning that not a single person has been killed as a result of volcanic activity in Iceland in the past two hundred years; people feel that they are prepared, so they are not prone to panic. Having said that, there is genuine concern about the possible disruption that Katla's next eruption could cause: its last eruption in 1918 released five times as much lava as the eruption at Eyjafjallajökull in 2010, which caused the closure of airspace in fifteen EU countries when it shot a 5.6-mile (9-km) plume of volcanic ash into the sky.

It wasn't all bad though. What many people feared would be a death knell to the country's tourism sector following the crushing economic downturn of 2008 actually proved to be an important turning point. Proving the old adage that there is no such thing as bad publicity, the eruption and the countless news stories that followed proved to be a major catalyst, resulting in a new boom in the country's tourism industry that played a real part in turning Iceland's struggling economy around.

The last volcano in Iceland's south to earn a mention is Hekla, or, as locals affectionately call it, the Gateway to Hell. During the last millennium Hekla has been responsible for producing the largest amount of lava the world over. When it last erupted in 2000, geologists made a novel discovery. They found that a three-mile (5-km) pyroclastic flow—a dense, fast-moving current of lava, ash, and hot gases, considered the most dangerous of volcanic phenomena—had emerged during the eruption that had not been thought to be produced by the class of volcano to which Hekla belongs. The crowds of curious spectators that flock to the vicinity to watch the show will now need to be kept much farther away, lest they be submerged under a current of molten subterranean sludge. And yet, Hekla's slopes are still enjoyed today for the excellent hiking. *Thetta reddast, thetta reddast …*

Svartifoss waterfall in Skaftafell, part of Vatnajökull National Park.

The East

The east of Iceland, or Austerland as it is known locally, receives far fewer visitors than the southern region. Those willing to make the journey—by domestic flight from Reykjavik to the town of Egilsstaðir, or ferry, bus, or a one-day drive on the Ring Road—are rewarded with awe-inspiring landscapes and can take part in numerous activities that are on offer. The region is home to Iceland's largest forest, Europe's vastest wilderness, and a glacier that covers almost 10 percent of the country's entire landmass.

For those who fly in, upon landing in Egilsstaðir, keep an eye open at the town's lake—it's home to the Lagarfljót worm, a giant, snake-like creature that lives in its depths. Mention of a "wonderful thing" in this

One of the many beautiful ice caves of Vatnajökull National Park.

lake appears in Icelandic folklore as far back as the
fourteenth century, but the seemingly not-so-mythical
creature was sighted as recently as 2012, only this time
it was caught on camera. For the nonbelievers, footage
of the apparent sighting is available on YouTube.

Travel about fifteen miles (25 km) southwest
from Egilsstaðir, and you will reach the forest of
Hallormsstaðaskógur. Prior to human settlement,
almost 40 percent of Iceland's landmass is thought to
have been covered by forest, most of it birch. As in
all industrial societies, however, human habitation,
animal rearing, and farming practices led to the near
total destruction of such woodlands. Birchwood in
particular has traditionally been an important source
of firewood, livestock fodder, and building material
in Iceland. Today, thanks to local efforts, the country's

forests have nearly quadrupled in size since the 1950s. Hallormsstaðaskógur now covers approximately three square miles (about 740 hectares) and provides a habitat for a large variety of birds, including year-round residents of ravens, common redpolls, wrens, and goldcrests, as well as hosting migratory redwings, Eurasian woodcock, and meadow pipits. The water in the streams here is drinkable, and there are twenty-five miles (40 km) of well-marked trails for those who enjoy hiking, as well as a fully serviced campsite.

For those who really like to get away from it all, a trip to Europe's largest wilderness may be in order. Located a thirty-minute drive southwest of Hallormsstaðaskógur, the Wilderness Center offers a perfect base for activities in the area—the vastest highlands of Northern Europe—including horse riding, angling, hiking, and even a cable car across a raging glacial river. The center is housed in a converted farmhouse and offers accommodation, cooked meals, hot pools, a sauna, and a small museum.

Continue southwest to reach the Vatnajökull National Park, a UNESCO World Heritage Site and a nature-lover's paradise. It is one of Iceland's three national parks, and covers almost a whopping 14 percent of the country's landmass. Contained within the borders of the park are volcanoes, glaciers, waterfalls, ice caves, and seemingly endless hiking trails of varying levels of difficulty. The Vatnajökull Glacier is the largest in Europe: it's so large that its ice cap is visible from space. Buried beneath the deep ice are mountains, lakes, and even eight subglacial volcanoes—indeed it is this co-existence of extremes that earned Iceland its moniker "Land of Fire and Ice." There are seven visitor centers spanning the different regions of the park, where you can pick up information on local routes, activities, and accommodation. These are all accessible from the Ring Road.

The North

Mighty waterfalls, dramatic mountains, forest-filled canyons, and teeming lakes—northern Iceland has a lot going for it. It also has some of the best skiing in the country, with six ski resorts dotted throughout the region. Those who make the six- to seven-hour drive from Reykjavik will not be disappointed. Flights from Reykjavik land in Akureyri, the vibrant capital of the north, where it is possible to connect to other airports across the region, including Grimsey Island, Húsavík, and Vopnafjörður in the far northeast.

While not as popular as the south, the north of Iceland has its own circuit of gems, known as the Diamond Circle, and has the added benefit of usually being far less crowded. One such gem is the Dettifoss Waterfall, Iceland's most powerful. Water runs along the Jökulsá á Fjöllum River from the Vatnajökull Glacier

Whale watching, Húsavík.

before eventually flowing into the Greenland Sea. At
the site of the waterfall, the icy glacial runoff is thrown
130 feet (40 meters) down, across a 340-foot- (100-meter-)
wide ledge—it's a magnificent sight. The waterfalls can
be accessed via Route 862 from the Ring Road, as well
as from Route 85, which follows the coastline. For those
in a four-wheel drive, an alternative but unpaved access
way via Route 864 takes you to the east side of the falls,
where an even better view is to be had—the west side
can sometimes be obscured by the rising spray and mist
of the water.

Other stops on the Diamond Circle include Lake
Mývatn, located around one hour from Akureyri in an
area of wetlands abundant with birds, fish, and magical
geological activity. Mývatn means "midges" in Icelandic,

and the area is full of them. Thankfully, they don't bite, and are just annoying. The area is full of excellent hikes and the geothermal Mývatn Nature Baths is a perfect resting place for weary legs. Another worthwhile stop on the trail is the forested horseshoe-shaped Ásbyrgi Canyon. According to myth, the canyon was created when the Norse god Odin's eight-legged horse touched the Earth with one of its hooves as it galloped across the sky. Stop at the coastal town of Húsavík to watch numerous species of whales, dolphins, and sea birds frolic in the Greenland Sea.

Iceland's best skiing is to be had in the northern region, principally at the Hlíðarfjall resort, located three miles (5 km) north of Akureyri, which is open from November to May. There are slopes to suit all levels of experience, and instructors to assist those trying skiing or snowboarding for the first time.

The Westfjords

The Westfjords peninsula is Iceland's least traveled region, and its most remote. The natural landscape is humbling in its vastness and beauty, and you can drive for hours without seeing the busloads of tourists that have become ubiquitous on the main circuit, or even another car. The area requires more time to explore than the other regions, however—probably a minimum of three days—and extensive planning is advised. A lot of driving is involved between the amenities and places of interest, but the views more than make up for it. Here, the journey is very much part of the experience.

You can reach the Westfjords by car, bus, ferry, or plane. There have been significant improvements to the region's main roads in recent years, and most are now paved, but many of the smaller roads that one must take to reach the sights are still dirt tracks, so a four-wheel drive is recommended. The main roads are kept clear during the winter, but extensive travel in the region is limited to the warmer months of May through October.

Only about 7,000 people live in the whole peninsula, the majority of them in the region's capital, Ísafjörður. This has been a trading post since the seventeenth century, and its economy today relies on the fishing industry and the small number of tourists who visit. The town hosts "I Never Went South," one of Iceland's most popular rock festivals, which is held at Easter time.

Among the highlights of the region is the Hornstrandir Nature Reserve, home to the arctic fox. Those who hike in the area may be treated to a close encounter with these inquisitive creatures, which, as a result of being protected, do not fear humans, but rather expect them to share their lunch with them. The sea cliffs of the reserve are home to millions of nesting birds every summer, among them puffins, northern gannets, razorbills, auks, guillemots, and kittiwakes. As in much of Iceland, all the natural running water found in the park is safe to drink. The best months to visit are June,

July, and August—the site is completely inaccessible over winter.

Other features of the region include the towering Dynjandi Waterfall. Many locals proclaim this as their favorite of all the country's waterfalls, and for good reason: water cascades down seven layers of rock totaling more than 300 feet (100 meters) in height. A visit to the southern beach of Rauðasandur at low tide on a sunny day will reveal six miles (10 km) of orange, red, and pink sand set against the surrounding black cliffs. It is well worth the drive!

SAFETY

Iceland is an exceptionally safe country for travel. Crime is very rare, and serious crime rarer still. So safe is it, in fact, that Iceland has now been ranked as the world's most peaceful country for twelve years in a row. The capital, Reykjavik, Hafnarfjörður, and Garðabær could be said to be the most "exciting," though to an outsider the goings-on might seem unremarkable. If you are interested to know what "funny business" goes on, the Reykjavik Police Force, Lögreglan, publishes a daily list of notable occurrences and offenses dealt with that day. There is no army in Iceland, and, as you might imagine, its law enforcement officers are unarmed too, save for pepper spray. Iceland's equivalent of the SWAT team, the

Viking Squad, is the only service to carry arms, and since the unit's establishment in 1982 it has only ever fired a single bullet.

No, the dangers travelers face in Iceland are not from its inhabitants, but rather from its unforgiving natural environment. Between avalanches and volcanic eruptions, the weather can be both extreme and notoriously changeable, particularly in the highlands. People can get caught out at any time of year—temperatures can drop suddenly, and blizzards appear seemingly out of nowhere. "If you don't like the weather, wait five minutes," the local saying goes. Bringing warm layers and a coat is advised at any time of year, as is checking the forecast before heading out.

There follow some common problems that can be encountered when traveling in Iceland, and suggestions of how to avoid them.

On the Roads

Most minor incidents involving travelers in Iceland take place on the roads. Driving becomes more dangerous when roads are wet or icy, as is often the case, particularly in the highlands and during the winter months. As such, the speed limit of 90 kmph (60 mph) on the main roads should be respected as a maximum, and you should be prepared to adjust your speed according to the weather conditions. You can check travel conditions before you hit the road at www.safetravels.is, where you can also share a copy of your itinerary so that the emergency services will know where to look for you if necessary.

Never stop on the road in order to look at the view or take a photo. Instead, pull over to the hard shoulder or to one of the designated viewing points that are usually found at regular intervals.

Highland roads require a four-wheel-drive vehicle, and are closed during the winter. Dirt tracks are the norm here, and are not suitable for inexperienced drivers at any time of year. When driving on these dirt tracks, keep your speed low—below 65 mph (40 kmph)—as it is easier to lose control here.

You will also need to ford rivers without bridges. When you come to a river, plan your route before crossing. Identify the point where the water is shallowest, which is usually where the river meanders. Calm water indicates depth. Drive slowly and steadily, below 3 mph (5 kmph). Stay in a low gear, and do not shift gears mid-crossing. Do not drive against the direction of the current, as it increases the possibility of water damage to the engine. Keep an eye out for signs along the riverbank for more information.

Insurance extras such as ash, sand, and gravel are recommended.

As previously mentioned, gas stations can be few and far between. Keep your car topped up, and make sure your payment card is PIN-ready, as this is how cashiers are set up to take payment. If your card is not PIN-ready, purchase prepaid gas vouchers from a gas station or supermarket before starting out. Breaking down is never fun, and it's much less so when it's cold and help is far away. Keep a supply of food in the car along with a few extra clothes for warmth. Pray to the Norse gods for protection.

For emergency assistance call 112, which operates in English.

Beaches

The waves on many of Iceland's popular beaches are volatile and unpredictable. Undercurrents can be extremely powerful, and during the winter the water is icy cold; hypothermia can set in after just a short time in the water. A number of tourists have tragically lost their lives after being swept away by waves that they either misjudged or did not see coming. One particularly risky spot is the popular black sand beach at Reynisfjara. Do not take your chances, even if the weather seems calm—"sneak" waves strike without warning. Keep a distance from the water, and don't turn your back on the waves for long.

Icebergs and Lagoons

Many accidents in Iceland happen because people do things that they shouldn't—and they know they shouldn't be doing them because there are signs warning them not to. One example is venturing on to the ice on lagoons, such as the Jökulsárlón Glacier Lagoon at the southern end of Vatnajökull National Park. It has happened more than once that a visitor has ignored the signs and ventured on to the ice. It can happen that a moment later he finds that the ice he is walking on detaches itself from the safety of the shore, and that he is now standing on an iceberg adrift in a pool of freezing glacial water. At this point the iceberg could capsize under his weight, and becoming trapped under this block of ice becomes a very real possibility. In short, heed the signs, stick to the paths, and stay off the ice.

Other places where it pays to be vigilant include the geothermal pits, where the surrounding mud can be very soft and give way, or an explosion of scalding hot water can occur without warning. Strong winds pose a risk on cliff edges and elsewhere. Large trucks have been blown off roads, and people can easily be blown off balance. It should also go without saying that the exploration of glaciers or ice caves without a guide is asking for trouble.

This basic level of knowledge and understanding, and a healthy respect for the forces of nature, will ensure that your trip in Iceland remains safe and trouble-free.

CHAPTER EIGHT

BUSINESS BRIEFING

Iceland's economy relies on three central pillars: fishing, manufacturing (mainly the production of aluminum and silicone), and tourism. The coronavirus outbreak in 2020 dealt a great blow to Iceland's tourism sector, which had previously experienced growth of almost 400 percent between the years of 2010 and 2019. Iceland's rate of unemployment, recently as low as 2.9 percent, has risen as a result of the fallout, though it remains to be seen to what extent it will be affected in the long run. While the tourism sector is expected to recover in due course, other areas of strength have come to the fore, among them the development of data centers, algae culture, life-science industries such as biotechnology and pharmaceuticals, and telecom services.

Across all sectors, Iceland's workforce is highly educated and adaptable. There is a reliable infrastructure—more than 90 percent of people have access to broadband Internet— and English is widely spoken to a high level. Entrepreneurial labor is encouraged, and the government has invested in a number of strategies to attract and remove barriers to foreign investment, which was recognized as a key driver in the recovery from the 2008 economic crash.

Given Iceland's size, access to government agencies and official bodies is relatively easy. Market-driven competition is highly valued, as is the concept of fair play. In general, business etiquette in Iceland is similar to that of other western European countries, with some differences, the most important of which are covered in this chapter.

THE ICELANDIC WORK ETHIC

Icelanders are not work shy. As mentioned in Chapter 6, they work more hours a week than people in any other country in Europe. Though a forty-hour working week is the legal limit, working overtime is the norm, and a forty-five-hour week is the average. Working life starts young in Iceland; many children take on a summer job in their early teens, and by the age of fifteen many are working part-time throughout the year, alongside their studies. This industriousness does not wane in later life: though the retirement age in Iceland is sixty-seven for both men and women, it is common for many people to continue working beyond this age and well into their seventies.

As many Icelanders are quick to point out, longer hours do not necessarily equate to higher productivity, and proponents of a shorter working week argue that reducing working hours would serve to promote overall productivity, as well as reduce the stresses and strains that the working week places on the worker, which are considerable.

Anyone looking for an explanation of Icelandic work habits today should consider the country's history: early settlers on the island were only able to succeed, indeed survive, by working hard in some very difficult and unforgiving conditions. Fishing, historically Iceland's main industry, is also extremely labor intensive, and requires long hours of work. Whether or not these conditions are still necessary today is an ongoing topic of discussion, but old habits die hard, and they remain valued and expected by society at large.

The island's history and harsh natural environment also hold clues to understanding two other traits that are relative when it comes to Icelandic working life: the value placed on independence, and self-reliance. Both traits make for a unique managerial model, and raise issues regarding teamwork and risk, which are discussed below.

LABOR UNIONS

The overwhelming majority of wage earners in Iceland belong to a labor (trade) union—79 percent, in fact. The significance of this figure becomes apparent when it is compared to the OECD average, a mere 17 percent. Most employee contracts are based on collective wage agreements, depending on the union and industry. These stipulate the required working conditions, working hours, wages, holidays, and more.

According to a recent survey carried out by the University of Iceland, public opinion is vastly in favor of the role that professional and labor unions play in the labor market, whether it be protecting workers' rights or negotiating wages and employment terms on behalf of their members. Eighty-seven percent of Icelanders agree that workers need strong unions to protect their interests, and only 5 percent hold the opinion that strong unions hurt the wider economy. As such, their place in the labor market is stable and likely to remain a permanent fixture.

In addition to offering legal services in situations where members are in dispute with their employers, most unions in Iceland also operate funds to support their members in the event that they should fall ill, or want to supplement their skills with further education.

GENDER REPRESENTATION

Gender equality is as actively pursued in Icelandic workplaces as it is in society at large (see Chapter 2), and, though there are still issues to overcome, the country has much to show for its efforts. Today it ranks among the top countries in the world for gender equality across all key measures, and is often in first place. For example, when it comes to educational attainment, more than 60 percent of university undergraduates are female, and at Master's level that figure rises above 70 percent. So successful, in fact, has the drive been to get women into higher education that many are now concerned at the record-low levels of male participation as a result.

When it comes to business, female participation is growing there too: half of those who sit the GMAT entrance exam that must be taken in order to study business related courses, such as an

Icelandic prime minister Katrin Jakobsdottir, 2020.

MBA program, are women. Representation in senior jobs has improved markedly in the last decade too. In 2020, 42 percent of management positions in the country were held by women, and a mandatory quota ensures that 40 percent of all company board members are female. Currently, forty-five percent of all Iceland's parliamentarians are women, and the country was the first democratic nation to install a female head of state when Vigdis Finnbogadottir was elected in 1980 (see page 41).

One of the few remaining hurdles in the Icelandic workplace is that of a gender pay gap that remains at approximately 14 percent, depending on the industry. By way of reference, the gender pay gap in the US in 2020 was 19 percent, so it is not doing badly, comparatively; but many in Iceland would like to see it eradicated entirely, and consequently the government has been working to drive this figure down further. In 2018, all companies with more than twenty-five employees had to prove that men and women received equal pay via an Equal Wage Management Standard, which would issue certification to companies that upheld the equal pay requirements. In 2020, certification became mandatory and companies without it now incur a daily fine. More than that, the government has committed to completely erasing the pay gap by the end of 2022.

COMMUNICATION AND DRESS

The way Icelanders communicate in a professional setting is very similar to the way they do so outside the workplace: informally and directly. In general, they are largely uninterested in small talk, and when they speak they don't often stray far from the point. Beginning a conversation with niceties is certainly acceptable, but these should not last as long as they do, say, in the Middle or Far East, where pre-business conversation is generally considered essential to building rapport. In Iceland, straightforwardness is key, and trust is built through displaying competence and reliability.

Address your Icelandic colleagues and counterparts, however senior, by their first names. Regardless of anyone's place in the pecking order, to address someone using "Mr.," "Miss," or "Mrs.," and their surname, would be unusual. Many Icelanders like to believe their society to be something of a classless utopia, free of the scourge of social hierarchy. Many others dispute this view, but whether it's true or not, the fact remains that Icelanders do not respond well to symbols or overt notions of rank or seniority. It's why the first Viking settlers fled from Norway; it's why they never gave up on independence despite centuries of foreign rule; and it's why they are still not part of the EU. It follows therefore that Icelandic workplaces are deeply egalitarian, and this is reflected in how colleagues communicate with one another.

The Icelanders take pride in their appearance and, depending on the industry, workplace dress will vary from smart, usually in the business, financial, and government sectors, to casual, in sectors such as advertising, design, and services. For men, in most cases, dress trousers, dress shirt, and a jacket is appropriate attire, and a tie and smart shoes should be worn for important meetings. For women, tailored trousers or skirt, and a top, or a dress are suitable.

MANAGERIAL STYLES

As we have seen, the Icelanders are not fond of overt hierarchy, and thus heavy top-down management styles will not get one far here. Icelandic managers know this well, and their approach is characterized by a distribution of power and delegation of tasks, the setting of personal example, employing an optimistic can-do attitude, and passion for the task at hand. They also have a flair for unique and out-of-the-box solutions to problems as they arise; Icelandic managers are at home in uncertainty, where the notions of *þetta reddast* and *vertíðarhugarfar* (see Chapter 2) encourage speedy decision-making and fast action, though this does not always result in a positive outcome, as a preference for risk can lead to carelessness and the setting of unrealistic goals.

TEAMWORK

It has been said that Icelanders are not good team players—as we have seen, independence is a supreme value. That said, the difficult natural environment has taught people here the importance of working in harmony and that doing so is to the benefit of all. As such, teamwork is by no means a foreign concept, but it relies on mutual trust and respect. These are earned through friendly conduct, a positive attitude, competence, and setting a personal example. Egalitarian by nature, all members of the team expect to be able to share their opinions and to air their concerns, regardless of seniority. Team leaders and managers will have the final say, but it is important that all are included in the decision-making process; if they are not, resentment is likely to build.

Once a decision has been made, employees are generally given enough responsibility to complete their tasks without unnecessary involvement by management—micromanaging is neither expected nor appreciated. The success of the team will be important to all its members, and each will work—often long hours—to achieve its goals.

PUNCTUALITY

In contrast to their Nordic neighbors, Icelanders are not well known for their timekeeping, but, in general, meetings begin within five to ten minutes of their scheduled time. A firm commitment to the *thetta reddast* mentality means that everything will work out fine, and a few minutes don't matter. However, if you, a visitor, want to earn your Icelandic partners' trust, you should make every effort to be punctual. If you do find yourself running late, letting your hosts know by message or phone call would be appreciated.

MEETINGS AND PRESENTATIONS

With Iceland's population being the size that it is, most individual companies are relatively small, and so it is quite likely that key decision-makers will be present at meetings. Though the meeting will be informal and generally relaxed, good preparation is vital. When setting up the meeting, stick to the twenty-four-hour clock to avoid any confusion that may be caused by terms such as "a quarter to" and the like.

Upon arriving at a meeting, a firm handshake while making eye contact is the welcome greeting for both male and female colleagues and counterparts. A further handshake should also be offered at the end of proceedings. Take care to extend the greeting to all those taking part. It is also suitable to exchange business cards on the first meeting. As previously mentioned, extended small talk is not necessary before getting down to business.

Discussions will be held in English, without a translator. Though most professionals in Iceland are comfortable speaking and working in English, attempts at humor should be kept to a minimum, at least in the initial meetings. It's not that Icelanders don't appreciate humor, but rather that things are likely to get lost in translation owing to missing cultural references. Self-deprecating humor in particular is not well appreciated. As mentioned above, people will be on a first-name basis all round, and all those taking part in the meeting will expect to be able to participate in discussions.

If you are required to make a presentation, it's advisable to keep things short and to the point. Clear, well-ordered, and concise points will keep people's attention. Speaking too quickly, attempts at humor, and complicated slides will do the opposite. There is no need to become self-conscious if, during your presentation, you notice that your listeners' faces are somewhat blank; they will be paying attention to what you are saying without necessarily communicating their engagement through body language or facial expressions. There should be an opportunity for questions at the end of the presentation to allow people to clarify points that they may not have fully understood.

Gift giving is not an expected part of business proceedings in Iceland. A small gift from your home country, however, would be appreciated, and would not cause offense.

WORKING IN ICELAND

All nationals of countries that are part of the European Economic Area (EEA) or European Free Trade Association (EFTA) are permitted to work in Iceland without a permit for up to three months, and are permitted to remain in Iceland for up to six months if they are looking for employment. Upon arrival, those staying for up to three months must make contact with Iceland Revenue and Customs (Skatturinn) who will allocate you a system ID number and, following that, a necessary tax card. A residence permit is required for EEA and EFTA nationals if they intend to stay beyond the initial three-month work period. Those who wish to work in Iceland for more than three months must submit an A-271 form via Registers Iceland (www.skra.is).

Nationals from countries outside the EEA and EFTA require a work permit in order to work in

Iceland, regardless of the length of time they intend to stay. Applications for work permits are made via the Directorate of Immigration (Útlendingastofnun). Once the Directorate of Immigration is satisfied that your application meets all the requirements, they will forward your application on to the Directorate of Labour (Vinnumálastofnun), which is responsible for issuing the relevant residency permit. More information on permits can be found on the Web site of the Directorate of Labour at www.vinnumalastofnun.is/en/work-permits.

Citizens of Denmark, Finland, Sweden, and Norway are permitted to stay and work in Iceland without a residence permit. Today, around 19 percent of Iceland's workforce is made up of foreign nationals, the vast majority of them hailing from Poland.

CHAPTER NINE

COMMUNICATING

LANGUAGE

Icelandic (*Íslenska*) is a window to the Nordic soul: there are twelve different words for snow, at least sixty different words for the devil, and not a single word for please. It is both an ancient and a modern language. Part of the Indo-European family, it closely resembles Old Norse, the North Germanic language first brought to the island by Viking settlers in the ninth and tenth centuries. While Old Norse was spoken throughout the Scandinavian kingdoms of Norway, Sweden, and Denmark (as well as parts of Scotland and northern England), the first settlers to arrive in Iceland came in the main from western Norway and brought with them the Old Norse dialect specific to their locale, known as West Old Norse. Remarkably, Icelandic has not developed all that much in the thousand years since then, and retains much of its vocabulary, grammar, syntax, and orthography. It is for this reason that Icelanders today can read and understand texts written as early as the eleventh century. It would be almost impossible for native English- or French-speakers today to read such early texts in their languages.

The Icelandic alphabet is comprised of Latin letters but has ten additional letters known locally as *séríslenskur*, or "uniquely Icelandic," to the chagrin of speakers of Faroese—another West Old Norse language—who use them too. Here is a basic description of how to pronounce these letters:

CAPITAL	LOWER CASE	PRONOUNCED
Á	á	a long "a", as in "are" or "arm"
Æ	æ	as in "eye"
É	é	as in "yet"
Í	í	as in "see"
Ó	ó	as in "oh"
Ö	ö	as in "urn"
Ð	ð	voiced "th," as in weather
Ý	ý	as in "little"
Ú	ú	as in "yew"
Þ	þ	unvoiced "th," as in thing

The letters "c," "q," and "w" are today found only in imported loan words, and the letter "z" was abolished in 1973—well, until pizza finally arrived in the late eighties. All vowels can be either long or short, depending on the consonants that follow them, and the stress is almost always placed on the first syllable of a word. Of all the Scandinavian languages, Icelandic today most closely resembles Faroese and Norwegian. Faroese-speakers can usually understand Icelandic-speakers, and vice versa—even if they do complain about a thick accent—while Norwegians, for the most part, cannot.

Danish used to be the lingua franca of all Scandinavian countries, and though it is still taught in Icelandic schools, English has largely taken over this role. So advanced and comfortable are young Icelanders with spoken English that many people today are worried about its ever-growing use at the expense of Icelandic, which they see as becoming slowly marginalized. The same *Íslenska* of the ancient Sagas that was scrawled on vellum in the twelfth century remained a unifying and distinguishing factor throughout the centuries of Danish rule, and many are concerned at what could happen were something so intimately connected to their sense of history and identity to fall into disuse. In addition, the speed with which lives are changing to being lived online, where English is essential and Icelandic barely features, is seen as a further threat to the survival of the language.

It is the Icelandic Language Institute (Íslensk málstöð) that has been tasked with stemming the tide against Icelandic's "digital minorritization"—the process by which a majority language in the real world becomes a minority language online and in digital spaces—as well as with keeping Icelandic contemporary and relevant. It does this principally by weeding out new foreign loan words and creating new Icelandic alternatives as replacements by compounding the roots of Old Norse words. Determined not to let new technology succeed in doing what hundreds of years of colonial rule could not, the Institute has come up with new words such as *tölva*, the Icelandic word for computer; made up of the root words *tala* (number) and *völva* (a female seer, or prophetess), it translates literally as "prophetess of numbers." Other fun tech-related words include *sjónvarp*, for television, which translates literally as "picture-thrower," and *friðþófur*, for a pager, which translates rather accurately as "thief of the peace."

While there aren't distinguishable dialects in Icelandic, there are certainly regional variations and accents. Their detection may be beyond the means of non-native speakers, but a local will immediately hear the difference between the hardy *Nordlenska* spoken around Akureyri and Lake Mývatn and the slightly softer *Sunnlenska* accent spoken in the south.

Learning the Language

Those who decide to learn Icelandic as a second language usually fall into one of two categories: linguists or masochists. Icelandic grammar is notoriously complex, and there is a dizzying array of rules—and then exceptions to those rules. Of the Scandinavian languages, Icelandic is considered the most difficult, and the most "conservative." For example, there are still three genders: masculine, feminine, and neuter. (Danish and Swedish have both long since whittled theirs down to two.) In Icelandic, the gender of a noun can usually be deduced from its ending, of which there are six main forms. To make things more interesting, all numbers, adjectives, and pronouns must match the gender of the nouns they are referring to. There are three voices—active, passive, and middle. There are strong and weak nouns, which each have four cases, as in German—nominative, genitive, dative, and accusative—but are complicated by numerous exceptions. There are also four divisions of verbs—strong, weak, reduplicating, and irregular— each with numerous categories of conjugation. Have we put you off yet? There are also no indefinite articles (like "a" or "an"), which is why you will notice that some Icelandic speakers are prone to omitting them when speaking or writing in English.

Those who have mastered the language, whether out of interest or necessity, will tell you that the rewards are ample: the ancient language is incredibly rich, and getting a handle on it is extremely gratifying. The reaction of locals to your heroic efforts will be the *rúsínan í pylsuendanum*—the raisin at the end of the sausage. Those who have worked their way to fluency will tell you that it's not much harder than learning other Germanic languages, and for those who are interested there are multiple online resources available, as well as both year-long and summer courses run by the University of Iceland, the University of Akureyri, and numerous language schools in Reykjavik and elsewhere.

For the casual learner who would like to dip a toe into Icelandic's icy waters, more helpful than memorizing declension tables will be to learn words, phrases, and sentences that can be used in particular situations. Here are a few basics to ease you in:

ENGLISH	ICELANDIC
Hello	Hæ / Halló
Good Day	Góðan daginn
What's up?	Hvað segir þú?
Good Evening	Góða kvöldið
Good Night	Góða nótt
Nice to meet you	Gaman að kynnast þér
What is your name?	Hvað heitir þú?

How are you?	Hvernig hefur þú það?
Yes	Já
No	Nei
Good	Góður (m) Góð (f)
Bad	Vondur (m) Vond (f)
Sorry/ Excuse me	Afsakið / Fyrirgefðu
Thank you	Takk
Thank you very much	Takk fyrir
Where is ...	Hvar er...
How do I get to ...	Hvernig kemst ég til...
One ticket to ..., thanks	Einn miða til ...,takk
I love this	Ég elska þetta
Beautiful	Fallegt
Delicious	Ljúfengt
How much?	Hversu mikið
One beer please	Einn bjór, takk
Do you accept credit cards?	Takið þið við krítarkortum?
Where is the bathroom?	Hvar er klósettið?
Goodbye	Bless (often "bless bless")

COMMUNICATION AND BODY LANGUAGE

By and large, the Icelanders are not pretentious, and will rarely take offense. Sometimes called "the Latinos of the North," some Icelanders have a certain unpolished charm that is unique to Scandinavia.

Those who can appreciate it for what it is will find their time spent among Icelanders both refreshing and easygoing.

When speaking, Icelanders are forthright and direct, to the point that some visitors can find them abrasive, particularly those coming from countries where smiling pleasantries are liberally dispensed. No, in Iceland, it is necessity that rules. As any Italian will demonstrate, gesticulating and animating your speech with your hands and with exaggerated looks is both expressive and enlivening—but it is not strictly necessary for communication. This is why you will rarely see Icelanders wave their hands around while speaking, or hear them raise their voices.

When it comes to greetings, a firm handshake is the norm, accompanied with eye contact. From the morning until around 6:00 p.m., *góðan daginn* (good day) is the usual greeting, after which *góða kvöldið* (good evening) is used. A handshake on leaving is just as usual, though not essential. Among good friends, women will often hug each other and kiss on the cheek, as may close friends of the opposite sex. Men who are close may also hug each other on meeting.

In typical northern European fashion, personal space is valued and respected. Standing too close to someone is likely to be considered unusual and may cause your interlocutor some discomfort. Except between intimates, there is very little in the way of arm holding or touching. Making eye contact while talking is perfectly acceptable, but it should be intermittent and not sustained.

HUMOR

Much like the weather, Icelandic humor can best be described as dark and gloomy. Particularly popular is *gálgahúmor*, gallows humor, which makes merriment of misfortune and laughter of despair. Could it be any other way when there are no more than four or five

By Hugleikur Dagsson, cartoonist and master of *gálgahúmor*.

hours of daylight for much of the year? Sarcasm is not the lowest form of wit in Iceland, it is a survival strategy, and it goes back hundreds of years; even the Sagas are full of dry, sardonic remarks.

Happily, that tradition is alive and well in modern Iceland. Pioneer of the Icelandic standup scene Jón Gnarr was voted in as mayor of Reykjavik in 2010. His campaign had initially begun as a joke, a mocking satirical gesture aimed at the political class for their handling of the 2008 economic crisis. Few were laughing when his party, the Best Party, actually won. Don't worry, Reykjavik survived, but the party did not, and disbanded at the next election in 2014. There are rumors that Gnarr may run for president next, though.

Standup performance and live comedy shows have grown in popularity in recent years and there is now a dedicated space in downtown Reykjavik for those who would like to sample the scene in English, called the Secret Cellar, where shows are held most nights of the week. Iceland's humorous take on life's bleak and dreary experiences is gaining international fans too. Comedian Ari Eldjarn's standup show "Pardon my Icelandic" was a hit on Netflix when it was released in 2020, and strips by cartoonist Hugleikur Dagsson continue to shock and amuse in equal measure.

MEDIA

Television production in Iceland is booming. Increased government investment in the arts coupled with an increased demand for new content as a result of the coronavirus pandemic meant that the release schedule for new films and television in 2021 was the busiest in history. Among them were thirteen new Icelandic films and eight new TV series.

Iceland's first television station was set up by the American military in 1951 and broadcast an English-language schedule from the Keflavik airbase. It wasn't until 1966 that broadcasts in Icelandic began by RÚV, Iceland's National Broadcasting Service, which had until then been limited to radio. According to Iceland's Broadcasting Act, the RÚV is obligated to promote Icelandic language and culture and to honor democratic rules, human rights, and freedom of expression. As mentioned in Chapter 6, RÚV cut transmission every Thursday until 1987 in order to encourage more physical and social activity among viewers. Similarly, until 1983, it would cease to broadcast for the whole month of July. TV license fees were scrapped in 2007 in favor of a public tax payable by all working adults.

Some in Iceland today believe public TV should be a thing of the past, while others recognize its role in bringing the nation together, as well as providing critical information and services during national emergencies and natural disasters. Some 95 percent of the population use RÚV's services at least once a week, so both its role in the dissemination of information and its level of influence are critical and not easily overlooked.

In addition to RÚV's two channels there is a handful of others that are privately run. Online streaming services, such as Netflix, HBO, Amazon Prime, and C-more, as well as YouTube, compete with traditional television channels.

The Press

Newspapers are alive and well in Iceland. The country's first newspaper was published in 1848 and it has since grown to become one of the most avid newspaper-reading nations in the world. Among the dozens of domestically published papers, the two most widely circulated are *Fréttablaðið* ("The Newspaper") and *Morgunblaðið* ("The Morning Paper"). The first is more closely aligned with the pro-European Social Democratic Alliance, while the latter has traditionally had a closer relationship with the Eurosceptic and conservative-leaning Independence Party, though its editorial horizons have broadened in recent years.

The level of journalism in Iceland is high, thanks in large part to the Union of Icelandic Journalists, which has worked hard toward the development and upholding of professional journalism standards.

The publication of its code, the "Rules of Ethics in Journalism," in 1988 was a turning point for the industry that had until then been subject to partiality and heavy party preference.

The English-language *Icelandic Review* is published bi-monthly and offers a daily news service online. The most active and comprehensive English-language news Web site is *Reykjavik Grapevine*. It is also an online hub for a great deal of travel-related information, including trip ideas, reviews, and an up-to-date database of site information, attractions, and amenities.

Morgunblaðið, one of Iceland's most popular daily newspapers.

INTERNET AND SOCIAL MEDIA

Eighty percent of Iceland may well be uninhabited wilderness, but the other 20 percent is better connected than anywhere else on the European Continent. When it comes to mobile and Internet infrastructure, Iceland is one of the world's most advanced countries: 98 percent of households are connected to the Internet via fiber-optic broadband. In addition, Iceland is steaming ahead with the development of a 5G network; in September 2020, Vodafone Iceland activated its first 5G transmitter with the intention of building a 5G network in the capital area over the following two years. Icelandic Smart Cities are very much on the horizon.

With near-unfettered access, Icelanders are frequent and enthusiastic Internet and social media users. In fact, according to recent data, all 100 percent of the population use the Internet, and more than 90 percent use some form of social media platform. This is unmatched anywhere in Europe. The love affair with social media on the island is all encompassing and not confined to any one age group; more than 80 percent of those of aged seventy and over report using one or another of the main platforms regularly. Facebook is by far the most popular platform on the island, with some 93 percent of people accessing the site on a regular basis. By way of comparison, only 67 percent

Social media: it comes for all.

of Americans report regular use of the platform. The
next most popular social media platform in Iceland is
Snapchat, followed by Instagram, and then Twitter.

Interestingly enough for a country as liberal as
Iceland (see Chapter Two)—and uniquely in Europe—
pornography is illegal there. The ban is not enforced,
though, and online pornography is neither blocked
nor specifically banned.

Happily, public Wi-Fi hotspots are widely available
throughout the country. However, for any short-term
visitors who plan on taking a road trip or venturing off

the beaten path, buying a pre-paid Sim card either on arrival at Keflavik airport or in Reykjavik is highly recommended. The country's largest mobile network operators are Síminn, Nova, and Vodafone. All offer prepaid Sim card options.

Iceland has a vibrant digital sphere, and almost all traditional media, including print, radio, and television, offer versions of their content online. Digital tools, including social media platforms, are widely used for social, political, and civic activism.

CONCLUSION

Despite its geographic isolation and limited population, the Icelanders have succeeded in building a society with high standards of living, education, gender and sexual equality, and ecological protection.

The country is also extremely safe. There is no army to speak of, its police force is largely unarmed, and mothers are happy to leave their babies napping in strollers on the street unattended. Instead, the only dangers are those posed by the natural environment, and these can almost always be avoided with common sense and a little forward planning.

Where problems do arise, help is to be found: a welfare system supports those who may need assistance, while a national rescue organization staffed entirely by volunteers is always on call.

The deeply Icelandic approach of taking things as they come while being ever-ready to respond and to reassess has evolved to meet the needs of island life at the tip of the Arctic Circle, while the value placed on self-reliance and independence that was passed down from the earliest settlers ensures that all difficulties are overcome, one way or another.

Unpretentious and unassuming, the Icelanders are as down to earth as they come. Whatever your reason for coming to Iceland, take the time to get to know the people who live here and you will discover a refreshing candor, an uncompromising fair-mindedness, and a deep love of the magnificent nature alongside which they live so well.

USEFUL APPS

Aurora For those chasing the Northern Lights—and for those who aren't—this app will let you know how likely you are to see them according to your location, and where you should head to if you want to have a better chance of catching them.

Craving Run by *The Reykjavík Grapevine* online portal, this app uses GPS to find the restaurants nearest to your location. Grapevine has also created the **Appy Hour** app, which can be used to find nearby bars running happy hours, making for a more affordable night out.

Hand Picked Iceland Curated countrywide recommendations for Eating, Sleeping, Culture, Shopping, Playing, and Kids' Activities.

Iceland Road App As well as providing road maps and routes, the Iceland Road App can be used throughout the country to locate nearby accommodation, restaurants, activities and places of interest.

Icelandic Sagas Immerse yourself in Iceland's literary heritage and get to know the key characters of the seminal works.

Iceland Travel Guide Created by Triposo, this app offers information on sights, hotels, restaurants, and bars in Reykjavik and beyond. Read background information and download maps for access when out of WiFi range.

Rakning C-19 Iceland's official Covid-19 contact tracing app. Hailed for its privacy features, Rakning C-19 will let you know if you have been in contact with a virus carrier so that you can take appropriate action.

Straeto Available in English, this is an essential app for anyone who wants to get around Reykjavik and the south without remortgaging their house for taxi fares.

Vedur Don't get caught out by Iceland's changeable and sometimes extreme weather. Download Vedur for up-to-the-minute, countrywide weather reports.

Vegagerdin Receive updates on road conditions before you set out on your journey. Owing to unpredictable weather conditions, roads can be subject to closures at any time of year, particularly during the winter, when excessive snowfall can make roads unusable.

Wapp An app for hikers. Wapp provides trail maps and information on each route, as well as photos so that you know what to expect. You can search trails according to difficulty and terrain, and download maps for offline use.

112 Iceland This app is run by Iceland's emergency services (phone number 112). The app can be used both to alert emergency services that you need assistance and as a check-in function that allows your location to be stored should you need to be located, say during a bout of extreme weather.

FURTHER READING

Byock, Jesse. *Viking Age Iceland*. London: Penguin, 2001.

Byock, Jesse. *The Prose Edda: Norse Mythology*. London: Penguin, 2005.

Karlsson, Gunnar. *Iceland's 1100 Years: History of a Marginal Society*. London: C. Hurst & Co., 2020.

Magnusson, Sigurdur Gylfi. *Wasteland With Words: A Social History of Iceland*. London: Reaktion Books, 2010.

Neijmann, Daisy. *Colloquial Icelandic: The Complete Course for Beginners*. Abingdon-on-Thames: Routledge, 2015.

Sigmundsdottir, Alda. *The Little Book of the Hidden People: Twenty stories of elves from Icelandic folklore*. Reykjavik: Little Books Publishing, 2019.

Smiley, Jane. *The Sagas of the Icelanders*. London: Penguin, 2005.

Stefansson, Hjorleifur Helgi. *Icelandic Folk Tales*. Cheltenham: The History Press, 2020.

Willson, Margaret. *Seawomen of Iceland: Survival on the Edge*. Seattle: University of Washington Press, 2019.

PICTURE CREDITS

INDEX